PENGUIN NATURE LIBRARY

General Editor: Edward Hoagland

THE OUTERMOST HOUSE

Henry Beston (1888–1968) was born in Quincy, Massachusetts. Following a New England boyhood of sea and shore, Beston attended Harvard College, and, after receiving his B.A. in 1909 and M.A. in 1911, moved to France, where he taught English at the University of Lyons. After serving as a volunteer in the First World War, Beston returned to the United States, where, in 1925, he purchased fifty acres along the great outer dunes of Cape Cod and began his solitary year of contemplation and observation of nature recorded in his most famous work, *The Outermost House.* In 1930, Beston married Elizabeth Coatsworth, poet and children's writer, and settled at Chimney Farm in Nobleboro, Maine. His works include *Herbs and the Earth* (1935), *The St. Lawrence River* (1941), and *Northern Farm: A Chronicle of Maine* (1948).

Robert Finch was born in New Jersey in 1943 and has lived in West Virginia, Massachusetts, Indiana, and Oregon. He graduated from Harvard College in 1967 and has taught at Oregon State, Carleton College, the Bread Loaf Writers' Conference, and Cape Cod Community College. Since 1972 he has lived with his family in Brewster, on Cape Cod, where he writes and clams full-time. His books include *Common Ground: A Naturalist's Cape Cod*, *The Primal Place*, and *Outlands: Journeys to the Outer Edges of Cape Cod*. He is currently editing *The Norton Book of Nature Writing*.

The Penguin Nature Library

THE OUTERMOST
HOUSE *A Year of Life*
on the Great Beach of Cape Cod

HENRY BESTON

INTRODUCTION BY
ROBERT FINCH

PENGUIN BOOKS

PENGUIN BOOKS
Published by the Penguin Group
Viking Penguin Inc., 40 West 23rd Street, New York, New York 10010, U.S.A.
Penguin Books Ltd, 27 Wrights Lane, London W8 5TZ, England
Penguin Books Australia Ltd, Ringwood, Victoria, Australia
Penguin Books Canada Ltd, 2801 John Street, Markham, Ontario, Canada L3R 1B4
Penguin Books (N.Z.) Ltd, 182–190 Wairau Road, Auckland 10, New Zealand

Penguin Books Ltd, Registered Offices:
Harmondsworth, Middlesex, England

First published in the United States of America by
Doubleday & Company, Inc., 1928
Published by Henry Holt and Company, Inc., 1949
Viking Compass edition published 1962
Reprinted 1963, 1964, 1965 (twice), 1966 (three times),
1967, 1968, 1969 (twice), 1970 (twice), 1971, 1973, 1975 (twice)
Published in Penguin Books 1976
Reprinted 1977, 1981, 1983, 1984, 1986
This edition with an introduction by Robert Finch
published in Penguin Books 1988
Published simultaneously in Canada

1 3 5 7 9 10 8 6 4 2

LIBRARY OF CONGRESS CATALOGING IN PUBLICATION DATA
Beston, Henry, 1888–1968.
The outermost house: a year of life on the great beach of Cape
Cod / Henry Beston; introduction by Robert Finch.
p. cm.—(Penguin nature library)
Originally published: New York: Doubleday, 1928.
1. Natural history—Massachusetts—Cape Cod. 2. Birds—
Massachusetts—Cape Cod. 3. Cape Cod (Mass.)—Description and
travel. 4. Beston, Henry, 1888–1968. 5. Naturalists—United
States—Biography. I. Title. II. Series.
QH105.M4B47 1988
508.744'92—dc19   87-36090
ISBN 0 14 017.012 X (pbk.)

Title page illustration from a woodcut by Hope Nash

Printed in the United States of America by
R. R. Donnelley & Sons Company, Harrisonburg, Virginia
Set in Caslon 540

THE
PENGUIN NATURE
LIBRARY

Nature is our widest home. It includes the oceans that provide our rain, the trees that give us air to breathe, the ancestral habitats we shared with countless kinds of animals that now exist only by our sufferance or under our heel.

Until quite recently, indeed (as such things go), the whole world was a wilderness in which mankind lived as cannily as deer, overmastering with spears or snares even their woodsmanship and that of other creatures, finding a path wherever wildlife could go. Nature was the central theater of life for everybody's ancestors, not a hideaway where people went to rest and recharge after a hard stint in an urban or suburban arena, and many of us still do swim, hike, fish, birdwatch, sleep on the ground, or paddle a boat on vacation, and will loll like a lizard in the sun any other chance we have. We can't help grinning for at least a moment at the sight of surf, or sunlight on a river meadow, as if remembering in our mind's eye paleolithic pleasures in a home before memories officially began.

It is a thoughtless grin because nature predates "thought." Aristotle was a naturalist, and, nearer to our own time, Darwin and Thoreau made of the close observation of bits of nature a lever to examine life in many ways on a large scale. Yet nature writing, despite its basis in science, usually rings with rhapsody as well—a belief that nature is an expression of God.

In this series we are presenting some nature writers of the past century or so, though leaving out great novelists like Turgenev, Melville, Conrad, and Faulkner, who were masters of natural description, and poets such as Homer (who was perhaps the first nature writer, once his words had been transcribed). Nature writing now combines rhapsody with science and connects science with rhapsody. For that reason it is a very special and a nourishing genre.

EDWARD HOAGLAND

INTRODUCTION

Majestic and mutilated, the great glacial scarp of Cape Cod's outer beach rises from the open Atlantic, separating it from Cape Cod Bay. Its many-colored sands and clays flow grain by grain, or in sudden shelving slabs, to replenish the shore below. The beach itself, broad and gently sloping in summer, short and steep in winter, arcs northward for over twenty miles, giving the walker a curved prospect two or three miles ahead at most. And always, coming onto the shore and re-forming it, with measured cadences in calm weather, with life-destroying fury during northeast gales, is the sea. Here, as Henry Beston put it, "the ocean . . . encounters the last defiant bulwark of two worlds." There is no other landscape like it anywhere.

This stretch of shoreline has been a remarkably fertile landfall for American nature writing. William Bradford, in his *Of Plymouth Plantation*, made it the subject of one of the first memorable evocations of the North American coast, that "wild and savage hue" which greeted the little band of English Puritan emigrés after their rough crossing of the Atlantic during the fall of 1620. Over the centuries an extraordinary number of essayists, poets, and novelists have written of its suggestive landscape. Few, if any, natural areas of comparable size on the continent have been written about so extensively and so well, perhaps in part because this meeting place of land and sea—of the gentle, human-scaled contours of the Cape's soft sands and the protean, formless wilderness of the open ocean—allows us to see what we need to see, providing us with the raw materials of personality and voice.

Henry Beston Sheahan was thirty-six years old when he first came to Coast Guard Beach (or Eastham Beach, as it was called then) in the summer of 1924. Though he had already published five books (including an account of his experiences as a volunteer in World War I and two volumes of fairy tales), he had not yet made a name for himself and was still casting about for his proper subject and style. After the war he had taught for a year at the University of Lyons and wandered about France, soaking up the Gallic culture he loved so much. But like that other American expatriate, William Faulkner, Beston had to return home, or near it, to find his true identity as a writer.

Though born in 1888 in Quincy, Massachusetts, home of the presidential Adamses, and a graduate of Harvard College, Beston was no Yankee. His father was a successful physician of Irish ancestry, his mother a French Catholic. He was raised bilingually and claimed to think in French as easily as English. This linguistic duality seems to have made him, like Conrad, particularly attuned to the cadences and sounds of written language.

As his career developed, Beston seemed to identify more and more with his French half. His first book, *A Volunteer Poilu*, was published under his given name, Henry Sheahan, but he subsequently adopted Beston as his professional name, after his maternal grandmother's family. He was a natty dresser. There is a picture of him, taken on the outer beach about 1927, which shows a tall, handsome man with classic Gallic features, sporting a clipped mustache, a French beret, and a dark double-breasted suit accented with a puffed white handkerchief. Thoreau took a flute with him to Walden; Beston brought a concertina to the beach.

Thoreau's famous visits to Cape Cod three-quarters of a century earlier had been undertaken with a typically Yankee sense of purpose: "Wishing to get a better view than I had yet had of the ocean, which, we are told, covers more than two-thirds of the globe . . ." Beston, on the other hand, seems to have been gradually drawn there by the force of an attraction he only slowly came to understand. In 1925 he bought some fifty acres of duneland on the barrier beach two miles south of the Eastham Life Saving Station. He designed and had built for him a two-room cottage which he named the Fo'castle. The house was small but not particularly Spartan. He intended it solely as a vacation retreat and "had no notion whatever of using the house as a dwelling place."

In September of the following year he went to spend two weeks there, but, "The fortnight ending, I lingered on, and as the year lengthened into autumn, the beauty and mystery of this earth and outer sea so possessed and held me that I could not go." He seemed to sense that here at last he might find his full expression as a writer, and so he stayed. In December 1926 he inscribed in his journal, in French, this statement of his subject and purpose:

> *La Nature, voilà mon pays.*
> *L'oeuvre—célébrer, révéler la mystère, la beauté,*
> *et la mystique de la Nature, du Monde Visible.*
> *Attacher ce sentiment à mon nom.*

> (Nature—there is my country.
> The work—to celebrate, to reveal the mystery,
> the beauty, and the rites of Nature, of the
> Visible World.
> To bind this feeling to my name.)

Despite this dedication of himself as a writer-naturalist (the phrase he used to describe himself), Beston seemed to have no clear idea of producing a book from his year of living on the beach. Not so with his fiancée, Elizabeth Coatsworth, herself a writer and a woman with formidable belief in and ambition for Henry's talents. He left the beach in the fall of 1927 with several notebooks full of material but no publishable manuscript. When he proposed setting a wedding date, Elizabeth replied, "No book, no marriage." *The Outermost House* was published in the fall of 1928; the Bestons were married the following June.

The Outermost House produced only modest initial sales, but its readership continued to grow. By 1949 it had gone through eleven printings, and in 1953 a French edition was published under the title *Une Maison au Bout du Monde* (*A House at the End of the World*). With the emergence of a post–World War II environmental literature, it began to achieve something of a cult status. Rachel Carson said that it was the only book that influenced her writing. In 1960 *The Outermost House* was cited by federal officials as one of the motivating forces in the creation of the Cape Cod National Seashore. It is now generally acknowledged as one of the classics of American nature writing, and each succeeding generation seems to have discovered anew the book's unique attraction.

Though written when Beston was middle-aged, *The Outermost House* is very much a young man's book, passionate and indulgent, full of a sense of discovery and self-discovery. Ever since *Walden*, American readers have been infatuated with romances of isolation, with solitary truth-seekers in the wilderness. Thoreau went to the Concord woods, he says, "to live deliberately, to front only the essential facts of life . . . to live deep and suck out all the marrow of life." There is something of the same sense of a quest for "essentials" and a vivid, tactile experience of life in Beston's explanation of why he decided to stay on the beach:

> The world today is sick to its thin blood for lack of elemental things, for fire before the hands, for water welling up from the earth, for air, for the dear earth itself underfoot. . . . The longer I stayed, the more eager was I to know this coast and to share its mysterious and elemental life.

Coupled with this eager youthful romanticism, however, is a mature and stable personality, one that has taken the measure of the world and knows where its allegiances lie. Compared with Thoreau's bristly and challenging stance towards "the mass of men," Beston's attitude is congenial and sociable. He may castigate our "civilization obsessed with power, which explains its whole world in terms of energy," but his posture toward the reader is inclusive, Whitmanesque, inviting us to share and loaf and explore with him.

Despite his canonization and the frequent quotation of his works by the conservation movement, Beston cannot be considered an original environmental thinker in the same category as, say, Aldo Leopold or Rachel Carson. Nor was he, like them, a trained scientist, or even an expert field-naturalist. He preferred poetic impressions to scientific accuracy. (Nearsighted, he rarely used his glasses. "When I don't use them," he claimed, "everything seems more beautiful, like a tapestry.") Many of his observations and interpretations, in fact, seem to spring more from imagination than from nature. How else, for instance, does one account for his description of ruddy turnstones in full breeding plumage on New Year's Day?

But Beston thought of himself first as a writer, rather than a naturalist, and it is in the imaginative qualities of *The Outermost House* that we must look to find the secret of his book's enduring appeal. He understood, as well as anyone before or after him, the psychic roots of our need for and response to wild nature. His primary achievement as a writer was to frame and shape that understanding with a remarkable vitality, immediacy, and sense of cosmic drama.

As a stylist, Beston was an extremely conscientious craftsman. We are told by his wife, "He sometimes spent an entire morning on a single sentence, unable to go on until he was completely satisfied with both words and cadence, which he considered equally important." The result was a richness of texture and a sense of rhythm unsurpassed in this genre. His are burnished, polished sentences, richly metaphoric and musical, that beg to be read aloud. Despite his Gallic affectations, Beston's style harkens back to the great English prose masters of the Jacobean age: John Donne, Thomas Browne, and the authors of the King James Bible. He often experiments with complex alliteration, mimetic rhythm, internal rhyme, and other devices of lyric poetry. Consider, for instance, the sense of interrupted rush conveyed in this description of wind-whipped dune grass:

> That intricacy of green, full-fleshed life, which billowed like wild wheat in the summer's southwest wind, has thinned away now to a sparse world of separate heads, each one holding, as in a fist, a clump of whitish and mildewed wires.

To express that sense of raw creation which he finds on the beach, he will not hesitate to reach for the climactic, Metaphysical phrase, portraying, for example, the migratory impulse in shorebirds as "the unknown and the distant articulate in the bright aërial blood." At the same time, few writers match him in conveying the precise feel of a sensory experience, whether it is that of stepping on a washed-up skate at night ("a huge unexpected something suddenly writhed horribly in the darkness under my bare foot") or simply noting the quality of illumination on an autumn evening ("the level and quiescent dust of light"). Some of the book's chapters, in fact, can be read as explorations into the nature of individual senses. "The Headlong Wave" attempts an almost musical analysis of the sound of surf; "Night on the Great Beach" is a rediscovery of the sense of touch; and "The Year at High Tide" celebrates the nose, still regarded, says Beston, as "something of an indelicate organ" by the English.

Above all, his descriptions tend to be kinesthetic, rich combinations of the observed and the felt, reflecting his belief that any full understanding of nature requires the full engagement of the observer with what he observes, with all senses healthy and receptive. His style, in other words, reflects his belief that "poetry is as necessary to comprehension as science."

The language of *The Outermost House*, however, does not exist for its own sake, but rather serves to heighten what is perhaps the book's most outstanding quality: its extraordinary sense of natural drama. Few volumes begin with such a sense of promise. Its memorable opening paragraphs, with their long rolling periods and stately incantatory rhythms, create at once a sense of vast geological time and of ancient ongoing conflicts. The technique is consciously cinematic. Beston pans in on his subject as an aerial camera might, from a distance of enormous space and time, gradually focusing in on his small stretch of beach. From the very start we have a sense of being drawn into some epic saga, a story of great heroic deeds acted out by figures larger than life:

Age by age, the sea here gives battle to the land; age by age, the earth struggles for her own, calling to her defense her energies and her creations, bidding her plants steal down upon the beach, and holding the frontier sands in a net of grass and roots which the storms wash free.

"Into the vast, bright days I go," he announces, and with him we enter a world in which even the most ordinary days are fraught with imminent adventure and dramatic moment. In the 1920s this outer shore was still the scene of much danger and tragedy. Shipwrecks and loss of life were common. A young surfman on his night patrol might stumble upon the body of his drowned father on the beach. Beston himself encountered real risk during his sojourn there, as when he rode out a fierce winter storm in his little house perched precariously above the pounding surf, a storm in which, he later confessed to a friend, "I almost died once or twice."

Despite the presence of such "dread elemental things" in the book, human drama is presented as a relatively minor part of a much larger and impersonal drama. Courage, daring, beauty, mystery, and suffering more often wear a nonhuman face in this world. Shorebirds wheel and flock in patterns of mysterious psychic connections; migrating monarch butterflies excite Beston's admiration and wonder by the sheer temerity of their enterprise; a doe, trapped in an ice-filled marsh, stands "resolute for life" through the darkness of a long winter night; a pigeon hawk flies out of a cut in the dunes "with a wretched junco gripped beneath him."

Yet even this nonhuman drama exists within a more comprehensive context. The restless sea and the mutable land seem to lend animation to all things on the beach. Even the humblest objects possess the power to come alive suddenly, to be incarnate with volition and incandescent with meaning. Stationary beach plants "jump from the dune rim to the naked slopes." Sand takes on a life of its own in the form of a "wind devil," "a brownish prism of burning, spinning and fantastic color." Chasing "a flying speck sailing landward out of the wrack," the author finds it to be "an autumn leaf, a maple leaf flat and drenched and red." A surfman, walking his night rounds in a thick fog, is overtaken by "a great, dark, bounding thing which moaned as it ran"—a monster which turns out to be a large empty barrel whose open bunghole whistled as it rolled up into the wind.

So strongly does Beston infuse his landscape with living and nonliving drama that when he claims that he was never bored, that "there was always something to do," we never doubt him. In one of the wonderful set pieces of the book, he describes how during a particularly savage winter storm the blackened skeleton of an ancient ship that had been buried for over a century in a dune "floated and lifted itself free . . . thus stirring from its grave and yielding its bones again to the fury of the gale." It is a marvelous event, but, we feel, not an odd one in this world where life and death are constantly changing and interchangeable.

Such vivid moments and images litter the beach of Beston's pages. Rarely are they fleshed out into complete vignettes and scenes. Rather, they surface like intense fragments of stories, dramatic phonemes. Incidents small and fragmentary take on sharp, but mo-

mentary, identity and significance. One of the most
common adjectives in the book is "fugitive." The
shore becomes a place of constant change, never complete, but ever fecund with meaning, "an odd blend
of illusion and reality." Nature is, for Beston, the un-
formed source of all human beauty, providing us with
the tropes and metaphors of human meaning.

Like so many great nature writers before and after
him, Beston uses the controlling metaphor of the natural year to structure his book. Much of the style,
imagery, and power of *The Outermost House* flows from
the author's central concept of his year on the beach
as a celebration of a fundamental and ongoing ritual.
"The natural year," he says, "is not so much a great
drama as a ritual." And again, "A year in outer nature
is the accomplishment of a tremendous ritual." Repeatedly he presents the natural phenomena of the
beach in deliberately ceremonial terms, as pageants of
symbolic figures moving across a sacred setting:

> great breakers born of fog swell and the wind rolled
> up the sands with the slow, mournful pace of stately
> victims destined to immolation.

Beston's images, which can often seem like indulgent,
stylistic bravura when taken separately, are carefully
chosen to place even the most humble events and
organisms within this cosmic ritual. A flock of small
shorebirds are "turned into a constellation of birds, a

fugitive pleiades whose living stars keep their chance positions." Strolling at night among bioluminiscent plankton washed up on the beach, he observes, "I walked in a dust of stars." Even the absence of insect life on the dunes in winter leads him to an intense poetic apprehension of the all-embracing solar cycles to which even the smallest and most buried life is connected:

> yet one feels them here, the trillion, trillion tiny eggs in grass and marsh and sand, all faithfully spun from the vibrant flesh of innumerable mothers, all faithfully sealed away, all waiting for the rush of this earth through space and the resurgence of the sun.

At the heart of this ritual is the image of the sun, and *The Outermost House* is, at its core, a book of sun-worship. More than a vivid record of changing natural drama, it is a consecration of the solar year, a ritual naming and chanting of its progress, a rededication of human perception and connection to its great wheeling harmonies.

"The adventure of the sun," Beston asserts, "is the great natural drama by which we live." Throughout the book the figure of the sun appears repeatedly as the principal actor and scene-changer of this drama: "The sun, descending the altar of the year, pauses ritually on the steps of the summer months"; "the great sun overflows; the year burns on"; "All these autumn weeks I have watched the great disk going south along the horizon of moorlands beyond the marsh"; "the turn of the sun's wheel, always the imperative, bright sun."

It may seem odd to contemporary readers to think of the natural year as a metaphor by which we live. As individuals, we have become far removed from direct participation in the patterns and particularities of the changing seasons. Insulated, air-conditioned, and jet-propelled, we have come to believe that we are largely independent of the earth's basic rhythms. If we think of the year metaphorically at all, it is as a source of sentimental song lyrics and greeting card verses, rather than as a vital, ongoing ritual that includes us.

Beston's unique strength as a nature writer lies in his ability to reconnect us emotionally and imaginatively to these primal, natural sources of our being, to link us to a world larger and more enduring than what he calls "our fantastic civilization." The importance and the lasting appeal of *The Outermost House*, I believe, is its power to remind us how much, in our computer age, we still rely on the earth's deep, constant rhythms, its basic integrity and equanimity. We continue to count on the safe and stable context that it provides, even as we tamper with and begin to rupture its basic systems. It allows us our freedom, to perform our daring and reckless feats of enterprise, growth, and exploitation. Yet for all our obsession with freedom, we want it as children want it and need it— within safe bounds. We want to know that, no matter how far out we walk, or how fast we race around the globe, the earth will be there to catch us if we slip and stumble, to lift us back from the brink of doom. The recurring cycles of the year, rooted in "the pilgrimages of the sun," are not simply entertaining phenomena, to be noted at our convenience and for our enjoyment, but signs that the cosmos is still intact, that we remain included in something larger and more reliable than our own short-lived enthusiasms. It is for this that we need to know that insects will hibernate, that turtles and warblers will migrate and return, that the tide will retreat, the ice let go, the earth tilt back toward the sun, and the grass reawaken.

This is why, despite the many new and exciting metaphors for viewing existence which science has given us over the past century—evolution, selfish genes, the Big Bang, the uncertainty principle, deep time, etc.—it is "the burning ritual of the year," as Beston calls it, which remains the basic form of nature writing, the one to which we return again and again, the perennial source of fundamental images for the shape and progress of our lives. We depend on it not only for biological survival, but for human meaning itself, as the raw material for our language and the terms by which we define ourselves. For human life, as Beston concludes, is itself a ritual:

> The ancient values of dignity, beauty and poetry which sustain it are of Nature's inspiration; they are born of the mystery and beauty of the world.

At the end of the book's penultimate chapter, there is a remarkable image of a naked swimmer in the surf. It is a beautiful, vigorous passage, worthy of Whitman, completely lacking in voyeurism. Simple in its description, it is yet a complex mixture of idealism and realism, which recognizes "the mystery of the human body and of how nothing can equal its rich and rhythmic beauty when it is beautiful or approach its forlorn and pathetic ugliness when beauty has not been mingled in or has withdrawn."

The dualism in this passage is found elsewhere throughout the book and helps to give it its peculiar strength. For Beston saw the Great Beach of Cape Cod, and by extension all of nature, as a place of dynamic and complementary opposites, of illusion and reality, beauty and terror, chance and law, the human and the "nothing human." In the image of the swimmer, "free for the moment of everything save his own humanity and framed in a scene of nature," Beston momentarily reconciled the conflicting claims of the individual and society and caught forever the ideal image of himself on the beach. Like all sojourners in the wilderness, however, he had to leave the place where he found his vision in order to convey it to us.

The year of *The Outermost House* ends in late summer, or what Beston called "The Year at High Tide." The book was also, as it turned out, the high tide of his life as a writer. Soon after his marriage he moved to Chimney Farm in Nobleboro, Maine, where he spent most of the rest of his life, rarely returning to the Cape. He wrote nine more nature books, including *Herbs and the Earth* (1935), *The St. Lawrence* (1942), and *Northern Farm* (1948), a chronicle of his life as a gentleman farmer. There are in these other books passages as good as anything he ever wrote (one thinks, for instance, of the opening of *Herbs and the Earth*). But never again did he achieve that sustained level of writing—with its seamless conjunction of subject and style, its total engagement with its material, its invigorating sense of liberation and breaking into identity—found in *The Outermost House*. After he wrote the Foreword to the 1949 edition, which has since become an integral part of the text, he published little else during the last two decades of his life.

Honors to the man and his book, however, continued to accrue. Beston received two honorary doctorates, and the American Academy of Arts and Sciences awarded him a medal for distinguished service in literature (previously awarded only to Robert Frost and T. S. Eliot). In the fall of 1964 he returned to Coast Guard Beach one last time for the dedication of his beach cottage as a National Literary Landmark. The Fo'castle, which he had given to the Massachusetts Audubon Society in 1960, had already been moved back from the eroding beach and would be moved again a few years later, making it the only traveling literary landmark in existence.

Henry Beston died in 1968. The cottage continued to be rented to Audubon members every summer until

1978. In February of that year a massive winter storm, comparable to the one he describes in the "Midwinter" chapter, swept the Fo'castle off its foundation and out to sea. All that was recovered were the brass plaque designating the cottage's landmark status and, ironically, the outhouse. The day after the storm I received a phone call from a friend, who asked, "Did you hear that the Outermost House perished?" Somehow it seemed fitting that its destruction should be referred to by a term usually reserved for thoughts, souls, and the principles of human liberty.

ROBERT FINCH

TO
MISS MABEL DAVISON
AND
MISS MARY CABOT WHEELWRIGHT

FOREWORD TO THE
ELEVENTH PRINTING

With the appearance of this edition of THE
OUTERMOST HOUSE, the book celebrates its twen-
tieth anniversary and an eleventh printing. The
text is unchanged, remaining what it was when
first set down in long hand on the kitchen table
overlooking the North Atlantic and the dunes,
the little room full of the yellow sunlight reflected from the sands and the great sound of the
sea.

It is the privilege of the naturalist to concern
himself with a world whose greater manifesta-
tions remain above and beyond the violences of
men. Whatever comes to pass in our human
world, there is no shadow of us cast upon the rising of the sun, no pause in the flowing of the winds
or halt in the long rhythms of the breakers hasten-
ing ashore. On the outer beach of the Cape, the
dunes still stand in their barrier wall, seemingly
much the same, but to the remembering eye somewhat reshaped by wind and wave. The little
house, to whom the ocean has been kind, has been

compelled by the hurricane winds to find a better foundation and build a new chimney, else all is with it as before. At the Coast Guard Station there are new activities and new faces, and the visitor will find there sons of the very men mentioned in this book. With such changes, however, the dune world is not concerned. In that hollow of space and brightness, in that ceaseless travail of wind and sand and ocean, the world one sees is still the world unharrassed of man, a place of the instancy and eternity of creation and the noble ritual of the burning year.

As I read over these chapters, the book seems to me fairly what I ventured to call it, "a year of life on the Great Beach of Cape Cod." Bird migrations, the rising of the winter stars out of the breakers and the east, night and storm, the solitude of a January day, the glisten of dune grass in midsummer, all this is to be found between the covers even as today it is still to be seen. Now that there is a perspective of time, however, something else is emerging from the pages which equally arrests my attention. It is the meditative perception of the relation of "Nature" (and I include the whole cosmic picture in this term) to the human spirit. Once again, I set down the core of what I continue to believe. Nature is a part of our humanity, and without some awareness and experience of that divine mystery man ceases to be man. When the Pleiades and the wind in the grass are no longer a part of the human spirit, a part of very flesh and bone, man becomes, as it were, a kind of cosmic outlaw, having neither the completeness and integrity of the animal nor the birthright of a true humanity. As I once said elsewhere, "Man can either be less than man or more than man, and both are monsters, the last more dread."

The author wishes to thank most gratefully the friends at Rinehart and Company whose good will makes possible this new edition of his book. He also wishes to thank, and again most gratefully, that staunch and discerning friend of those who write about Nature in America, Professor Herbert Faulkner West of Dartmouth College.

HENRY BESTON

January, 1949

CONTENTS

THE OUTERMOST HOUSE

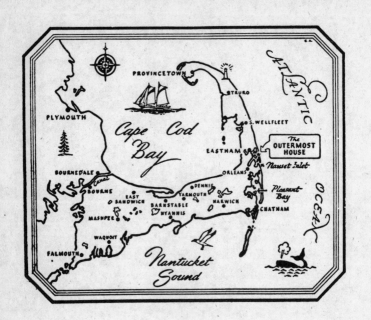

THE OUTERMOST HOUSE

Chapter I

THE BEACH

I

East and ahead of the coast of North America, some thirty miles and more from the inner shores of Massachusetts, there stands in the open Atlantic the last fragment of an ancient and vanished land. For twenty miles this last and outer earth faces the ever hostile ocean in the form of a great eroded cliff of earth and clay, the undulations and levels of whose rim now stand a hundred, now a hundred and fifty feet above the tides. Worn by the breakers and the rains, disintegrated by the wind, it still stands bold. Many earths compose it, and many gravels and sands stratified and intermingled. It has many colours: old ivory here, peat here, and here old ivory darkened and enriched with rust. At twilight, its rim lifted to the splendour in the west, the face of the wall becomes a substance of shadow and dark descending to the eternal unquiet of the sea; at dawn the sun rising out of ocean gilds it with a level silence of light which thins and rises and vanishes into day.

At the foot of this cliff a great ocean beach runs north and south unbroken, mile lengthening into mile. Solitary and elemental, unsullied and remote, visited and possessed by the outer sea, these sands might be the end or the beginning of a world. Age by age, the sea here gives battle to the land; age by age, the earth struggles for her own, calling to her defence her energies and her creations, bidding her plants steal down upon the beach, and holding the frontier sands in a net of grass and roots which the storms wash free. The great rhythms of nature, to-day so dully disregarded, wounded even, have here their spacious and primeval liberty; cloud and shadow of cloud, wind and tide, tremor of night and day. Journeying birds alight here and fly away again all unseen, schools of great fish move beneath the waves, the surf flings its spray against the sun.

Often spoken of as being entirely glacial, this bulwark is really an old land surfaced with a new. The seas broke upon these same ancient bounds long before the ice had gathered or the sun had fogged and cooled. There was once, so it would seem, a Northern coastal plain. This crumbled at its rim, time and catastrophe changed its level and its form, and the sea came inland over it through the years. Its last enduring frontier roughly corresponds to the wasted dyke of the cliff. Moving down into the sea, later glaciations passed over the old beaches and the fragments of the plain, and, stumbling over them, heaped upon these sills their accumulated drift of gravels, sand, and stones. The warmer sea and time prevailing, the ice cliff retreated westward through its fogs, and presently the waves coursed on to a new, a transformed and lifeless, land.

So runs, as far as it is possible to reconstruct it in general terms, the geological history of Cape Cod. The east and west arm of the peninsula is a buried area of the ancient plain, the forearm, the glaciated fragment of a coast. The peninsula stands farther out to sea than any other portion of the Atlantic coast of the United States; it is the outermost of outer shores. Thundering in against the cliff, the ocean here encounters the last defiant bulwark of two worlds.

II

The cliff I write of and the bordering beach face the Atlantic on the forearm of the Cape. This outer earth is now scarce more than a great dyke or wall some twenty-five miles long and only three and four miles wide. At Province-town it rises from the sea, beginning there in a desert of dunes and sand plains of the ocean's making. These sands curve inland toward the continent, bending toward Plymouth even as a hand may be bent down at the wrist, and Provincetown harbour lies in the curve of palm and fingers. At Truro, the wrist of the Cape— the forearm simile being both exact and in-escapable—the land curve falls from the east and west down through an arc to the north and south, and the earth cliff begins and rises rather suddenly to its greatest elevation. South by east from the Highland Light to Eastham and Nauset Coast Guard Station, the rampart fronts the sea, its sky line being now a progress of long undulations, now a level as military as a battle-ment, hollows and mounded hills here and there revealing the barren moorland character of the country just above. At Nauset, the cliff ends, the sea invades the narrowing land, and one enters the kingdom of the dunes.

The cliff ends, and a wall of ocean dunes carries on the beach. Five miles long, this wall ends at a channel over whose entrance shoals the ocean sweeps daily into a great inlet or lagoon back of the dunes, an inlet spaced with the floors of tidal islands and traced with winding creeks—the inlet of Eastham and Orleans. Very high tides, covering the islands, sometimes turn this space into bay. Westward over the channels and the marshland one looks to the uplands of the Cape, here scarce a good two miles wide. At Eastham, the land is an open, rolling moor. West over this lies Cape Cod Bay. A powerful tribe of Indians, the Nausets, once inhabited this earth between the seas.

Outermost cliff and solitary dune, the plain of ocean and the far, bright rims of the world, meadow land and marsh and ancient moor: this is Eastham; this the outer Cape. Sun and moon rise here from the sea, the arched sky has an ocean vastness, the clouds are now of ocean, now of earth. Having known and loved this

land for many years, it came about that I found
myself free to visit there, and so I built myself a
house upon the beach.

My house stood by itself atop a dune, a little
less than halfway south on Eastham bar. I
drew the home-made plans for it myself and it
was built for me by a neighbour and his car-
penters. When I began to build, I had no notion
whatever of using the house as a dwelling place.
I simply wanted a place to come to in the
summer, one cosy enough to be visited in winter
could I manage to get down. I called it the
Fo'castle. It consisted of two rooms, a bedroom and a kitchen-living room, and its dimen-
sions over all were but twenty by sixteen. A
brick fireplace with its back to the wall between
rooms heated the larger space and took the chill
off the bedroom, and I used a two-burner oil
stove when cooking.

My neighbour built well. The house, even as
I hoped, proved compact and strong, and it was
easy to run and easy to heat. The larger room
was sheathed, and I painted the wainscoting
and the window frames a kind of buff-fawn—a
good fo'castle colour. The house showed, perhaps, a somewhat amateur enthusiasm for

windows. I had ten. In my larger room I had seven; a pair to the east opening on the sea, a pair to the west commanding the marshes, a pair to the south, and a small "look-see" in the door. Seven windows in one room perched on a hill of sand under an ocean sun—the words suggest cross-lights and a glare; a fair misgiving, and one I countered by the use of wooden shutters originally meant for winter service but found necessary through the year. By arranging these I found I could have either the most sheltered and darkened of rooms or something rather like an inside out-of-doors. In my bedroom I had three windows—one east, one west, and one north to Nauset light.

To get drinking water, I drove a well pipe directly down into the dune. Though the sea and the beach are alongside, and the marsh channels course daily to the west, there is fresh water here under the salty sand. This water varies in quality, some of it being brackish, some of it sweet and clear. To my great delight, I chanced upon a source which seems to me as good water as one may find here anywhere. Beneath the floor, the pipe descended into a bricked-up and covered pit housing a pet-cock through which I drained the water from the pump in freezing weather (On bitter days I simply pumped a few pails full and stood them in the sink, and drained the pump immediately.). I had two oil lamps and various bottle candlesticks to read by, and a fireplace crammed maw-full of drift-wood to keep me warm. I have no doubt that the fireplace heating arrangement sounds demented, but it worked, and my fire was more than a source of heat—it was an elemental presence, a household god, and a friend.

In my larger room, I had a chest of drawers painted an honest carriage blue, a table, a wall bookcase, a couch, two chairs, and a rocker. My kitchen, built yacht fashion all in a line, stood at my southern wall. First came a dish and crockery cupboard, then a space for the oil stove—I kept this boxed in when not in use— then a shelf, a porcelain sink, and the corner pump. Blessed pump! It never failed me or in-dulged in nerves.

Using a knapsack, I carried my supplies on my own shoulders. There is no road through the dunes, and, even if there were, no one would have made deliveries. West of the dunes, it is true, there exists a kind of trail on which Fords

may venture, but even the most experienced of
the villagers are wary of it and tell of being mired
there or stuck in the sand. Nevertheless, my
lumber came by this trail, and now and then I
could get my oil cans carried down by a neighbour who had a horse and cart. These helps,
however, were but occasional, and I counted
myself fortunate to have had them at all. My
knapsack remained the only ever-ready wagon of
the dunes. Twice a week, by arrangement, a
friend met me at Nauset Station with a car,
took me shopping to Eastham or Orleans, and
brought me back again to Nauset. And there I
would pack my milk and eggs and butter and
rolls—being very careful as to which was sitting
on which—and strike off down the beach along
the breakers.

The top of the mound I built on stands scarce
twenty feet above high-water mark, and only
thirty in from the great beach. The coast
guards at Nauset, a scant two miles away, were
my only neighbours. South lay the farther
dunes and a few far-away and lonely gunning
camps; the floor of marsh and tide parted me on
the west from the village and its distant cottages;
the ocean besieged my door. North, and north

alone, had I touch with human things. On its solitary dune my house faced the four walls of the world.

My house completed, and tried and not found wanting by a first Cape Cod year, I went there to spend a fortnight in September. The fortnight ending, I lingered on, and as the year lengthened into autumn, the beauty and mystery of this earth and outer sea so possessed and held me that I could not go. The world to-day is sick to its thin blood for lack of elemental things, for fire before the hands, for water welling from the earth, for air, for the dear earth itself underfoot. In my world of beach and dune these elemental presences lived and had their being, and under their arch there moved an incomparable pageant of nature and the year. The flux and reflux of ocean, the incomings of waves, the gatherings of birds, the pilgrimages of the peoples of the sea, winter and storm, the splendour of autumn and the holiness of spring—all these were part of the great beach. The longer I stayed, the more eager was I to know this coast and to share its mysterious and elemental life; I found myself free to do so, I had no fear of being alone, I had something of a field naturalist's inclination; presently

I made up my mind to remain and try living for a
year on Eastham Beach.

III

The sand bar of Eastham is the sea wall of the
inlet. Its crest overhangs the beach, and from
the high, wind-trampled rim, a long slope well
overgrown with dune grass descends to the
meadows on the west. Seen from the tower at
Nauset, the land has an air of geographical
simplicity; as a matter of fact, it is full of hollows,
blind passages, and amphitheatres in which the
roaring of the sea changes into the far roar of a
cataract. I often wander into these curious
pits. On their floors of sand, on their slopes, I
find patterns made by the feet of visiting birds.
Here, in a little disturbed and claw-marked
space of sand, a flock of larks has alighted; here
one of the birds has wandered off by himself;
here are the deeper tracks of hungry crows;
here the webbed impressions of a gull. There
is always something poetic and mysterious to me
about these tracks in the pits of the dunes; they
begin at nowhere, sometimes with the faint impression of an alighting wing, and vanish as suddenly into the trackless nowhere of the sky.

Below the eastern rim the dunes fall in steeps of sand to the beach. Walking the beach close in along these steeps, one walks in the afternoon shade of a kind of sand escarpment, now seven or eight feet high and reasonably level, now fifteen or twenty feet high to the top of a dome or mound. In four or five places storms have washed gullies or "cuts" clean through the wall. Dune plants grow in these dry beds, rooting themselves in under old, half-buried wreckage, clumps of dusty miller, *Artemisia stelleriana*, being the most familiar green. The plant flourishes in the most exposed situations, it jumps from the dune rim to the naked slopes, it even tries to find a permanent station on the beach. Silvery gray-green all summer long, in autumn it puts on gold and russet-golden colourings of singular delicacy and beauty.

The grass grows thickest on the slopes and shoulders of the mounds, its tall leaves inclosing intrusive heads and clumps of the thick-fleshed dune goldenrod. Still lower down the slope, where the sands open and the spears rise thin, the beach pea catches the eye with its familiar leaf and faded topmost bloom; lower still, on desert-like floors, are tussock mats of poverty grass and the flat green stars of innumerable spurges. The only real bushes of the region are beach plum thickets, and these are few and far between.

All these plants have enormously long taproots which bury themselves deep in the moist core of the sands.

The greater part of the year I have two beaches, one above, one below. The lower or tidal beach begins at mean low water and climbs a clean slope to the high-water mark of the average low-course tide; the upper beach, more of a plateau in form, occupies the space between high water and the dunes. The width of these beaches changes with every storm and every tide, but I shall not be far out if I call them both an average seventy-five feet wide. Unseasonable storm tides and high-course tides make of the beach one vast new floor. Winter tides narrow the winter's upper beach and often sweep across it to the dunes. The whole beach builds up in summer as if each tide pushed more and more sand against it out of the sea. Perhaps currents wash in sand from the outer bars.

It is no easy task to find a name or a phrase for the colour of Eastham sand. Its tone, moreover, varies with the hour and the seasons. One friend says yellow on its way to brown, another speaks of the colour of raw silk. Whatever colour images these hints may offer to a reader's mind, the colour of the sand here on a June day is as warm and rich a tone as one may find. Late in the afternoon, there descends upon the beach and the bordering sea a delicate overtone of faintest violet. There is no harshness here in the landscape line, no hard Northern brightness or brusque revelation; there is always reserve and mystery, always something beyond, on earth and sea something which nature, honouring, conceals.

The sand here has a life of its own, even if it is only a life borrowed from the wind. One pleasant summer afternoon, while a high, gusty westerly was blowing, I saw a little "wind devil," a miniature tornado six feet high, rush at full speed out of a cut, whirl itself full of sand upon the beach, and spin off breakerward. As it crossed the beach, the "devil" caught the sun, and there burst out of the sand smoke a brownish prism of burning, spinning, and fantastic colour. South of me, the dune I call "big dune" now and then goes through a curious performance. Seen lengthwise, the giant has the shape of a wave, its slope to the beach being a magnificent fan of purest wind-blown sand, its westward slope a descent to a sandy amphitheatre. During a recent winter, a coast guard key post was erected on the peak of the dune; the feet of the night patrols trod down and nicked the crest, and presently this insignificant notch began to "work" and deepen. It is now eight or nine feet wide and as many deep. From across the marshes, it might be a kind of great, roundish bite out of the crest. On windy autumn days, when the sand is still dry and alive, and westerly gusts and currents take on a genuine violence, the loose sand behind the dune is whirled up by the wind and poured eastward through this funnel. At such times the peak "smokes" like a volcano. The smoke is now a streaming blackish plume, now a thin old-ivory wraith, and it billows, eddies, and pours out as from a sea Vesuvius.

Between the dunes and the marshes, an ir-regular width of salt-hay land extends from the sand slopes to the marshier widths of tidal land along the creeks. Each region has its own grasses, the meadows being almost a patchwork of competing growths. In the late summer and the autumn the marsh lavender, thin-strewn but straying everywhere, lifts its cloud of tiny sun-faded flowers above the tawny, almost deer-coloured grasses. The marsh islands beyond are but great masses of thatch grass rising from floors of sodded mud and sand; there are hidden pools in these unvisited acres which only sunset reveals. The wild ducks know them well and take refuge in them when stalked by gunners.

How singular it is that so little has been written about the birds of Cape Cod! The peninsula, from an ornithologist's point of view, is one of the most interesting in the world. The interest does not centre on the resident birds, for they are no more numerous here than they are in various other pleasant places; it lies in the fact that living here, one may see more kinds and varieties of birds than it would seem possible to discover in any one small region. At Eastham, for instance, among visitors and migrants, residents and casuals, I had land birds and moor birds, marsh birds and beach birds, sea birds and coastal birds, even birds of the outer ocean. West Indian hurricanes, moreover, often catch up and fling ashore here curious tropical and semi-tropical forms, a glossy ibis in one storm, a frigate bird in another. When living on the beach, I kept a particularly careful lookout during gales.

I close this chapter with what seems to me the most interesting detail for a naturalist's ear. Eastham bar is only three miles long and scarce a quarter of a mile wide across its sands. Yet in this little world Nature has already given her humbler creatures a protective colouration. Stop at the coast guard station and catch a locust on the station lawn—we have the maritime locust here, *Trimerotropsis maritima harris*—and, having caught him, study him well; you will find him tinted with green. Go fifty feet into the dunes and catch another, and you shall see an insect made of sand. The spiders, too, are made of sand—the phrase is none too strong—and so are the toads that go beach combing on moonlit summer nights. One may stand at the breakers' edge and study a whole world in one's hand.

So, choosing to remain upon the beach, I look forward to October and winter and the great migrations. Earliest autumn and September now enclose the earth.

My western windows are most beautiful in early evening. On these lovely, cool September nights the level and quiescent dust of light which fills the sky is as autumnal in its colouring as the earth below. There is autumn on the earth and autumn overhead. The great isles of tawny orange smouldering into darkness, the paths of the channels stilled to twilight bronze, the scarlet meadows deepening to levels of purple and advancing night—all these mount, in exhalation of colour, to the heavens. The beam of Nauset, entering my northern casement, brushes a recurrent pallor of light across a part of my bedroom wall. A first flash, a second flash, a third flash, and then a little interval as the dark sector of the lens travels between the Fo'castle and the flame. On bright moonlit nights, I can see both the whitewashed tower and the light; on dark nights, I can see only the light itself suspended and secure above the earth.

It is dark to-night, and over the plains of ocean the autumnal sky rolls up the winter stars.

Chapter II

AUTUMN, OCEAN, AND BIRDS

I

There is a new sound on the beach, and a greater sound. Slowly, and day by day, the surf grows heavier, and down the long miles of the beach, at the lonely stations, men hear the coming winter in the roar. Mornings and evenings grow cold, the northwest wind grows cold; the last crescent of the month's moon, discovered by chance in a pale morning sky, stands north of the sun. Autumn ripens faster on the beach than on the marshes and the dunes. Westward and landward there is colour; seaward, bright space and austerity. Lifted to the sky, the dying grasses on the dune tops' rim tremble and lean seaward in the wind, wraiths of sand course flat along the beach, the hiss of sand mingles its thin stridency with the new thunder of the sea.

I have been spending my afternoons gathering

driftwood and observing birds. The skies being clear, noonday suns take something of the bite out of the wind, and now and then a warmish west-sou'westerly finds its way back into the world. Into the bright, vast days I go, shouldering home my sticks and broken boards and driving shore birds on ahead of me, putting up sanderlings and sandpipers, ringnecks and knots, plovers and killdeer, coveys of a dozen, little flocks, great flocks, compact assemblies with a regimented air. For a fortnight past, October 9th to October 23d, an enormous population of the migrants has been "stopping over" on my Eastham sands, gathering, resting, feeding, and commingling. They come, they go, they melt away, they gather again; for actual miles the intricate and inter-crisscross pattern of their feet runs unbroken along the tide rim of Cape Cod.

Yet it is no confused and careless horde through which I go, but an army. Some spirit of discipline and unity has passed over these countless little brains, waking in each flock a conscious sense of its collective self and giving each bird a sense of himself as a member of some migrant company. Lone fliers are rare,

and when seen have an air of being in pursuit
of some flock which has overlooked them and
gone on. Swift as the wind they fly, speeding
along the breakers with the directness of a runner
down a course, and I read fear in their speed.
Sometimes I see them find their own and settle
down beside them half a mile ahead, sometimes
they melt away into a vista of surf and sky, still
speeding on, still seeking.

The general multitude, it would seem, consists
of birds who have spent the summer somewhere
on the outer Cape and of autumn reinforcements
from the north.

I see the flocks best when they are feeding on
the edge of a tide which rises to its flood in the
later afternoon. No summer blur of breaker
mist or glassiness of heat now obscures these
outer distances, and as on I stride, keeping to
the lower beach when returning with a load, I
can see birds and more birds and ever more birds
ahead. Every last advance of a dissolved
breaker, coursing on, flat and seething, has those
who run away before it, turning its flank or
fluttering up when too closely pursued; every
retreating in-sucked slide has those who follow
it back, eagerly dipping and gleaning. Having

fed, the birds fly up to the upper beach and sit there for hours in the luke-cold wind, flock by flock, assembly by assembly. The ocean thunders, pale wisps and windy tatters of wintry cloud sail over the dunes, and the sandpipers stand on one leg and dream, their heads tousled deep into their feathers.

I wonder where these thousands spend the night. Waking the other morning just before sunrise, I hurried into my clothes and went down to the beach. North and then south I strolled, along an ebbing tide, and north and south the great beach was as empty of bird life as the sky. Far to the south, I remember now, a frightened pair of semipalmated sandpipers did rise from somewhere on the upper beach and fly toward me swift and voiceless, pass me on the flank, and settle by the water's edge a hundred yards or so behind. They instantly began to run about and feed, and as I watched them an orange sun floated up over the horizon with the speed and solemnity of an Olympian balloon.

The tide being high these days late in the afternoon, the birds begin to muster on the beach about ten o'clock in the morning. Some fly over from the salt meadows, some arrive flying along the beach, some drop from the sky. I startle up a first group on turning from the upper beach to the lower. I walk directly at the birds—a general apprehension, a rally, a scutter ahead, and the birds are gone. Standing on the beach, fresh claw marks at my feet, I watch the lovely sight of the group instantly turned into a constellation of birds, into a fugitive pleiades whose living stars keep their chance positions; I watch the spiralling flight, the momentary tilts of the white bellies, the alternate shows of the clustered, grayish backs. The group next ahead, though wary from the first, continues feeding. I draw nearer; a few run ahead as if to escape me afoot, others stop and prepare to fly; nearer still, the birds can stand no more; another rally, another scutter, and they are following their kin along the surges.

No aspect of nature on this beach is more mysterious to me than the flights of these shore-bird constellations. The constellation forms, as I have hinted, in an instant of time, and in that same instant develops its own will. Birds which have been feeding yards away from each other, each one individually busy for his individual body's sake, suddenly fuse into this new volition and, flying, rise as one, coast as one, tilt their dozen bodies as one, and as one wheel off on the course which the new group will has determined. There is no such thing, I may add, as a lead bird or guide. Had I more space I should like nothing better than to discuss this new will and its instant or origin, but I do not want to crowd this part of my chapter, and must therefore leave the problem to all who study the psychic relations between the individual and a surrounding many. My special interest is rather the instant and synchronous obedience of each speeding body to the new volition. By what means, by what methods of communication does this will so suffuse the living constellation that its dozen or more tiny brains know it and obey it in such an instancy of time? Are we to believe that these birds, all of them, are *machina*, as Descartes long ago insisted, mere mechanisms of flesh and bone so exquisitely alike that each cogwheel brain, encountering the same environmental forces, synchronously lets slip the same mechanic ratchet? or is there some psychic relation between these creatures? Does some current flow through them and between them as they fly?

Schools of fish, I am told, make similar mass changes of direction. I saw such a thing once, but of that more anon.

We need another and a wiser and perhaps a more mystical concept of animals. Remote from universal nature, and living by complicated artifice, man in civilization surveys the creature through the glass of his knowledge and sees thereby a feather magnified and the whole image in distortion. We patronize them for their incompleteness, for their tragic fate of having taken form so far below ourselves. And therein we err, and greatly err. For the animal shall not be measured by man. In a world older and more complete than ours they move finished and complete, gifted with extensions of the senses we have lost or never attained, living by voices we shall never hear. They are not brethren, they are not underlings; they are other nations, caught with ourselves in the net of life and time, fellow prisoners of the splendour and travail of the earth.

The afternoon sun sinks red as fire; the tide climbs the beach, its foam a strange crimson; miles out, a freighter goes north, emerging from the shoals.

II

It chanced that on a mild September morning, as I was standing a moment at a window looking west over the marshes and the blue autumnal creeks, an alarm of some kind began to spread among the gulls. The incoming tide had already crowded the birds back on the higher gravel banks and bars, and from these isles, silvery cloud by cloud, I saw the gulls rise and stream away to the southward in a long, fugitive storm of wings. They were flying, I noticed, unusually low. Interested to see what had thus disturbed them, I stepped out a moment to the pinnacle of my dune. As I stood there staring after the vanishing gulls and questioning the sky, I saw far above the birds, and well behind them, an eagle advancing through the heavens. He had just emerged from a plume of hovering cloud into the open blue, and when I saw him first was sailing south and seaward on motionless wings, seeming to follow in the great sky the blue course of a channel far below.

There are sand bars at the mouth of Nauset harbour; many gulls feed there between the tides, and the gulls from the marsh joined forces with this gathering. As the eagle approached the bars, I looked to see if he would descend or fly out to sea. But no; at the harbour's entrance he turned south, aligned his flight with the coast line, and disappeared.

During the autumn I saw this same bird half a dozen different times. I could tell when he was about by the terror of the gulls. Yet this eagle --for a bald eagle, *Haliætus leucocephalus leucocephalus*, I believe him to have been—is, as Mr. Forbush says, "by nature a fish eater." I never saw him pay the slightest attention to the fugitives; nevertheless, he may well have a fancy for gulls when they are plump and he is hungry. At any rate, they fear him. There are always a few black-backed or "minister" gulls mingled in with the herring gulls upon these flats, and these burly giants, I noticed, sought refuge with the rest.

Eagles are by no means rare upon Cape Cod. The birds arrive here as coast-wise visitors, find the region to their liking, and establish themselves in various favourite domains. They fish in our sandy bays and inlets; they have rather a fancy for the more isolated Cape Cod ponds. Seen at close range, the bald eagle is a dusky brownish bird with a pure-white head, neck, and tail. I never had a near view of this Eastham visitor, but one of the coast guardsmen roused him up one day from a thicket close by the head of a creek running up into the moors—he heard a sudden noise of brush and great wings, he said, and, turning round, he saw the eagle rising free of the scrub and the bright leaves.

Ever since I came to live here on Cape Cod, I have been amazed at the number of land-bird migrants I have encountered on the dunes. I expected to see sandpipers on the beach and scoters in the surf, for they are coast-wise folk but I did not expect to see the red-breasted nut-hatch rise out of the September dunes, or find the charming black-and-yellow warbler sitting on the ridgepole of the Fo'castle, his black-tipped tail feathers turned to the Atlantic. But perhaps I had best begin at the beginning and tell how the sparrows and the warblers came down to us this autumn by the coast.

Various new sparrows were the first strangers to arrive. There are summer sparrows here, a great abundance of them, for the marsh and meadow land west of the dunes is the natural habitat of many species. Walk through these grass-lands on a summer's day, and you will see singles and flocks break from the sunburned stubble ahead, some to drop and hide again farther on, others to watch you from the coast-guard wires. Song sparrows are notably abundant, for these pleasant singers frequent both the marshes and the dunes; but the seaside sparrow keeps more to the marsh rim and the salt-hay mowings, the sharp-tailed sparrow fancies the wheel ruts of the hay carts, and the odd little grasshopper sparrow, *Coturniculus savannarum passerinus*, trills into the burning sundowns the two faint notes of his curious and poignant insect song.

Early in September Hudsonian curlews arrived in Eastham marsh, and to see them I began going to Nauset through the meadows instead of by the beach. High September tides were then covering both marsh and meadow land, and, as I pushed on each afternoon, the curlews rose from close beside the inundated road, and, circling, called to other curlews; I could hear, when I listened, the clear reply. And then there would be silence, and I would hear the sound of autumn and the world, and perhaps the faint withdrawing roar of ocean beyond the dunes. When I reached the wider meadows on these days, I found the stubble mobbed with sparrows; the population had doubled in a week.

Flocks of fox sparrows were feeding everywhere; I whirred up groups of savannah sparrows and families of white-throats; a solitary white-headed sparrow watched me from the concealment of a bush. It was a silent throng. I heard faint *"tsips"* and *"chips"* of alarm as I passed—nothing more. Love-making was over and done, and all were importantly busy with the importance of their lives.

On the 24th and the 25th there was wind and rain, and on the 27th I saw the first of the warblers.

The weather had cleared, and I had risen early and begun to get breakfast. It is my custom here to sit facing the sea, and I was moving over my table when I noticed a small bird of some kind foraging about in the grass before the house. I could not see him well at first, for he had entered into the grass as into a thicket, but presently out he came, pushing through the stalks, and I watched him from the window unsuspected. This first arrival was a Canadian warbler. Steely ash-gray above, yellow below, and with a broad band of black spots between his yellow throat and yellow belly, he was a charming bit of life. Over the pale sand, in and out of the tawny-white roots, in and out of the variegations of morning light he moved, picking up seeds while a sea wind shook the tops of the dying grass above his head. Presently, in search of still more food, he turned the corner of the house, and when I went out after breakfast he had gone.

Then came, all in one week, a Wilson's warbler (a female, probably), the black-and-yellow warbler, and a chestnut-sided warbler. The birds were singles, they travelled along the dunes, they fed on the fallen seeds. In October I saw in one day five myrtle warblers; a pair of these lingered a week near Fo'castle dune. Then came juncos and a raid of pigeon hawks. The juncos, like the warblers, foraged on the dunes, and the hawks hunted them there for an hour or so before the dawn. I went exploring one morning while Nauset was still flashing into a sullen, cold, and overclouded world, and saw a pigeon hawk rise unexpectedly out of the cut to the north with a wretched junco gripped beneath him. Flying seaward through the cut, the hawk carried his captive to the beach, found himself a sheltered nook close along the dune wall, stood at attention for a moment, and then unbent and ate.

I saw various other migrant land birds as well, but I shall not dwell upon them, for the listing and cataloguing of species seems to me of less interest than their arrival by sea. This outer arm of Cape Cod, as I have already explained, stands thirty miles or so out from the continental main, yet there are land birds, little birds, going south along it as casually as so many arctic geese. Writing here this cloudy morning, with a great confused roaring of breakers in my ears, I call to mind the Wilson's warbler, the female, I saw a fortnight ago, and I wonder where it was that she forsook her familiar earth for the grey ocean, an ocean she perhaps had never seen. What a gesture of ancient faith and present courage such a flight is, what a defiance of circumstance and death— land wing and hostile sea, the fading land behind, the unknown and the distant articulate and imperious in the bright, aërial blood.

But who shall say by what sea routes these landsmen reach the Cape? Some species, I

imagine, cross Massachusetts Bay, their jump-
ing-off place being north of Boston (Cape Ann
or Ipswich perhaps); some may cross over from
the South Shore at a point well north of Cape
Cod Bay, others undoubtedly come directly
down from Maine. The wooded archipelago of
Maine is a famous place for warblers. It is
quite possible that the species I have mentioned
may have followed some great river to the sea,
the Kennebec or the Penobscot, perhaps, and
crossed from the river mouth directly over to
Cape Cod. The Highland Light bears south
$\frac{3}{4}$ west (true) from Seguin at the mouth of the
Kennebec, and is separated from it by only 101
miles of open water. The birds could manage
this easily.

All over the world land migrants go great
distances over open water. Numbers of birds,
for instance, migrating back and forth between
Europe and North Africa cross the Mediterranean
twice a year, and in our own hemisphere there
are flights across the Gulf of Mexico and movements between the West Indies and our south
Atlantic states.

Late in October there came an easterly gale,
and in the afternoon, when the tide was high, I

put on oilskins and went out to see the surf.
About a mile to the north of the Fo'castle, as I
was trudging on across the rain, I saw just ahead
and close over the breakers a flying speck sailing
landward out of the wrack, and even as I stared,
it fell to the beach in danger of the waves. I
ran ahead, then, and picked the thing up just
as a slide of foam was about to overflow it, and
found it to be an autumn leaf, a maple leaf flat
and drenched and red.

Mid-October and the land birds have gone.
A few sparrows linger in the marshes. The plum
bushes have lost their leaves. Walking the
beach, I read winter in the new shapes of the
clouds.

III

Western cloud, dark substance of cloud,
gathered at the wintry horizon of the short-lived
days making them even shorter with the false
sundown of its rim. Now come the sea fowl and
the wild fowl to the beach from the lonely and
darkening north, from the Arctic Ocean and the
advancing pack, from the continental fragments
and great empty islands that lie between the
continent and the pole, from the tundra and the

barrens, from the forests, from the bright lakes, from the nest-strewn crevices and ledges of Atlantic rocks no man has ever named or scaled. Over the round of earth, down from the flattened summit, pour the living streams, bearing south the tribes and gathered nations, the peoples and flocks, the clans and families, the young and the old. And the dying grasslands, the October snows, and the forests fall behind, and presently the nations behold a first far glint of the sea.

There are many streams, and it is said that two of the greatest bear down upon Cape Cod. A first river, rising in the interior of Alaska, flows southeast across Canada to the Atlantic; on this stream move birds from the north woods and the Canadian lakes together with birds from the north barrens and the arctic isles and half lands; a second stream, rising in the shadow of the pole, flows south along the coast past Greenland and the bays of Labrador—on this move the hardy arctic folk who get their living from the tides. Many species are common to both streams. Somewhere north of the Cape, perhaps round and about the mouth of the St. Lawrence, these streams immix their multitudes,

and south to New England moves the great
united flood, peopling with primeval life the
seacoasts and the sky.

Ducks enter the channels, some flying in from
the bay, others from the outer ocean, geese
settle at sundown in the golden skin of the
western coves, coveys of winter yellow-legs circle
in the gloom, and hide when disturbed in the
taller salt grasses between the meadows and the
creeks. At nightfall and at daybreak I hear
birds talking. Strangers in rubber boots and
khaki uniforms now visit my domain, and every
Saturday afternoon I look with philosophy
through my western windows to a number of
tufts of grass disguised as gunners.

Now that I have settled down here for the
winter, I find myself becoming something of a
beach comber. Every once in a while, when I
chance to look seaward, I spy an unknown
something or other rising and falling, appearing
and disappearing in the offshore surges, and at
this sight the beach comber in me wakes. All
kinds of things "come ashore" on these vast
sands, and even the most valueless have an air
of being treasure trove. The mysterious something moving from the swells into the breakers

may be nothing but a smelly bait tub washed overboard from some Gloucester fisherman, or a lobster pot, or a packing case stencilled with a liner's name; but in the sea or on the beach a mile ahead it is something for nothing, it is the unknown, it is hope springing eternal in the human breast. The other day I found myself thoughtfully examining a U. S. Navy blue undress jumper which lay flat and soggy and solitary on the lower beach. It was not, in its day, an unfamiliar garment, and I have an old friend in the village who occasionally dons a rather good one he found just south of the light. Alas, the cloth was rotted and the jumper much too small. But I cut off and saved the buttons.

Now, while I stood there slicing off the buttons, I chanced to look up a moment at the southern sky, and there for the first and still the only time in my life, I saw a flight of swans. The birds were passing along the coast well out to sea; they were flying almost cloud high and travelling very fast, and their course was as direct as an arrow's from a bow. Glorious white birds in the blue October heights over the solemn unrest of ocean—their passing was more than music, and from their wings descended the old loveliness of earth which both affirms and heals.

IV

The last two weeks in October see the peak of the autumnal visitations. In November and December the stream from the inland shrinks, but the coast-wise stream, continuing to flow, brings us down a rare and curious world. Of this I shall write at greater length, for I found it of enormous interest.

Here, approaching the end of my notes on birds and autumn, I chance to remember that one of the strangest and most beautiful of the migrations over the dunes was not a movement of birds at all but of butterflies. There came a morning early in October which ripened, as the sun rose higher, into a rather mild and September-like day; the wind was autumnal, I recall, and from the north by west, but the current was both mildly warm and light. As it was a day to be spent out-of-doors, soon after ten o'clock I went out round the back of the Fo'castle into the sunlight and began to work there on a bin I was putting together out of driftage. I looked about, as I always do, but nothing in the landscape chanced to take my eye. Sawing and hammering, I worked for about three quarters of an hour, and then downed tools to take a moment's rest.

During the hour, a flight of twenty or more large orange-and-black butterflies had arrived in the region of the dunes. It was a flight, yet were the individuals far apart. There was at least an eighth of a mile between any two; some were on the dunes, some were on the salt meadows, three were on the beach. Their movements were casual as the wind, yet there was an unmistakable southerly pull drawing them on. I tried to catch one of the travellers on the beach, and though I count myself a fair runner, it was no easy work keeping up with his turns and erratic doublings. I wished him no ill; I simply wanted to have a better look at him, but he escaped me by rising and disappearing over the top of a dune. When I reached the same top after a scramble up a steep of sand, the fugitive was already a good eighth of a mile away. I went back to my carpentry with an increased respect for butterflies as fliers.

An entomologist with whom I have been in correspondence tells me that my visitors were undoubtedly specimens of the monarch or milkweed butterfly, *Anosia plexippus*. In early autumn adults gather in great swarms and move in a generally southward direction, and it is believed (but not proved) that New England specimens go as far as Florida. The following spring individuals (not swarms) appear in the North apparently coming from the South. We do not know—I am quoting this paragraph almost verbatim—whether these are returning migrants or whether they are individuals that had not previously been in the North. We do know that none of the fall migrants had previously been in the South.

The butterflies of Eastham remained upon the dunes the rest of the morning. I imagine that they were in search of food. Between half-past twelve and half-past one they melted away as mysteriously as they had come, and with them went the last echo of summer and the high sun from the dunes. And that day I finished my bin and filled it and began to build a wall of seaweed round the foundation of my house. A cricket sang as I worked in the mild afternoon, alive and hardy in his cave under my driftwood mountain, and beyond this little familiar sound of earth I heard the roar of ocean filling the hollow space of day with its inexorable warning.

Chapter III

THE HEADLONG WAVE

I

This morning I am going to try my hand at something that I do not recall ever having encountered either in a periodical or in a book, namely, a chapter on the ways, the forms, and the sounds of ocean near a beach. Friends are forever asking me about the surf on the great beach and if I am not sometimes troubled or haunted by its sound. To this I reply that I have grown unconscious of the roar, and though it sounds all day long in my waking ears, and all night long in my sleeping ones, my ears seldom send on the long tumult to the mind. I hear the roar the instant I wake in the morning and return to consciousness, I listen to it a while consciously, and then accept and forget it; I hear it during the day only when I stop again to listen, or when some change in the nature of the sound breaks through my acceptance of it to my curiosity.

They say here that great waves reach this coast in threes. Three great waves, then an indeterminate run of lesser rhythms, then three great waves again. On Celtic coasts it is the seventh wave that is seen coming like a king out of the grey, cold sea. The Cape tradition, however, is no half-real, half-mystical fancy, but the truth itself. Great waves do indeed approach this beach by threes. Again and again have I watched three giants roll in one after the other out of the Atlantic, cross the outer bar, break, form again, and follow each other in to fulfilment and destruction on this solitary beach. Coast guard crews are all well aware of this triple rhythm and take advantage of the lull that follows the last wave to launch their boats.

It is true that there are single giants as well. I have been roused by them in the night. Waked by their tremendous and unexpected crash, I have sometimes heard the last of the heavy overspill, sometimes only the loud, withdrawing roar. After the roar came a briefest pause, and after the pause the return of ocean to the night's long cadences. Such solitary titans, flinging their green tons down upon a quiet world, shake beach and dune. Late one September night, as I sat reading, the very father of all waves must have flung himself down before the house, for the quiet of the night was suddenly overturned by a gigantic, tumbling crash and an earthquake rumbling; the beach trembled beneath the avalanche, the dune shook, and my house so shook in its dune that the flame of a lamp quivered and pictures jarred on the wall.

The three great elemental sounds in nature are the sound of rain, the sound of wind in a primeval wood, and the sound of outer ocean on a beach. I have heard them all, and of the three elemental voices, that of ocean is the most awesome, beautiful, and varied. For it is a mistake to talk of the monotone of ocean or of the monotonous nature of its sound. The sea has many voices. Listen to the surf, really lend it your ears, and you will hear in it a world of sounds: hollow boomings and heavy roarings, great watery tumblings and tramplings, long hissing seethes, sharp, rifle-shot reports, splashes, whispers, the grinding undertone of stones, and sometimes vocal sounds that might be the half-heard talk of people in the sea. And not only is the great sound varied in the manner of its making, it is also constantly changing its tempo, its pitch, its accent, and its rhythm, being now loud and thundering, now almost placid, now furious, now grave and solemn-slow, now a simple measure, now a rhythm monstrous with a sense of purpose and elemental will.

Every mood of the wind, every change in the day's weather, every phase of the tide—all these have subtle sea musics all their own. Surf of the ebb, for instance, is one music, surf of the flood another, the change in the two musics being most clearly marked during the first hour of a rising tide. With the renewal of the tidal energy, the sound of the surf grows louder, the fury of battle returns to it as it turns again on the land, and beat and sound change with the renewal of the war.

Sound of surf in these autumnal dunes—the continuousness of it, sound of endless charging, endless incoming and gathering, endless fulfilment and dissolution, endless fecundity, and endless death. I have been trying to study out the mechanics of that mighty resonance. The dominant note is the great spilling crash made by each arriving wave. It may be hollow and booming, it may be heavy and churning, it may be a tumbling roar. The second fundamental sound is the wild seething cataract roar of the wave's dissolution and the rush of its foaming waters up the beach—this second sound *diminuendo*. The third fundamental sound is the endless dissolving hiss of the inmost slides of foam. The first two sounds reach the ear as a unisonance—the booming impact of the tons of water and the wild roar of the up-rush blending—and this mingled sound dissolves into the foam-bubble hissing of the third. Above the tumult, like birds, fly wisps of watery noise, splashes and counter splashes, whispers, seethings, slaps, and chucklings. An overtone sound of other breakers, mingled with a general rumbling, fells earth and sea and air.

Here do I pause to warn my reader that although I have recounted the history of a breaker —an ideal breaker—the surf process must be understood as mingled and continuous, waves hurrying after waves, interrupting waves, washing back on waves, overwhelming waves. Moreover, I have described the sound of a high surf in fair weather. A storm surf is mechanically the same thing, but it *grinds*, and this same long, sepulchral grinding—sound of utter terror to all mariners—is a development of the second fundamental sound; it is the cry of the breaker water roaring its way ashore and dragging at the sand. A strange underbody of sound when heard through the high, wild screaming of a gale.

Breaking waves that have to run up a steep tilt of the beach are often followed by a dragging, grinding sound—the note of the baffled water running downhill again to the sea. It is loudest when the tide is low and breakers are rolling beach stones up and down a slope of the lower beach.

I am, perhaps, most conscious of the sound of surf just after I have gone to bed. Even here I read myself to drowsiness, and, reading, I hear the cadenced trampling roar filling all the dark. So close is the Fo'castle to the ocean's edge that the rhythm of sound I hear oftenest in fair weather is not so much a general tumult as an endless arrival, overspill, and dissolution of separate great seas. Through the dark, mathematic square of the screened half window, I listen to the rushes and the bursts, the tramplings, and the long, intermingled thunderings, never wearying of the sonorous and universal sound.

Away from the beach, the various sounds of
the surf melt into one great thundering sym-
phonic roar. Autumnal nights in Eastham village
are full of this ocean sound. The "summer
people" have gone, the village rests and pre-
pares for winter, lamps shine from kitchen
windows, and from across the moors, the great
levels of the marsh, and the bulwark of the dunes
resounds the long wintry roaring of the sea.
Listen to it a while, and it will seem but one
remote and formidable sound; listen still longer
and you will discern in it a symphony of breaker
thunderings, an endless, distant, elemental can-
nonade. There is beauty in it, and ancient terror.
I heard it last as I walked through the village on
a starry October night; there was no wind, the
leafless trees were still, all the village was abed,
and the whole sombre world was awesome with
the sound.

II

The seas are the heart's blood of the earth.
Plucked up and kneaded by the sun and the
moon, the tides are systole and diastole of
earth's veins.

The rhythm of waves beats in the sea like a

pulse in living flesh. It is pure force, forever embodying itself in a succession of watery shapes which vanish on its passing.

I stand on my dune top watching a great wave coursing in from sea, and know that I am watching an illusion, that the distant water has not left its place in ocean to advance upon me, but only a force shaped in water, a bodiless pulse beat, a vibration.

Consider the marvel of what we see. Somewhere in ocean, perhaps a thousand miles and more from this beach, the pulse beat of earth liberates a vibration, an ocean wave. Is the original force circular, I wonder? and do ocean waves ring out from the creative beat as they do on a quiet surface broken by a stone? Are there, perhaps, ocean circles so great and so intricate that they are unperceived? Once created, the wave or the arc of a wave begins its journey through the sea. Countless vibrations precede it, countless vibrations follow after. It approaches the continent, swings into the coast line, courses ashore, breaks, dissolves, is gone. The innermost waters it last inhabited flow back in marbly foam to become a body to another beat, and to be again flung down. So it goes night and day, and will go till the secret heart of earth strikes out its last slow beat and the last wave dissolves upon the last forsaken shore.

As I stand on my dune top, however, I do not think of the illusion and the beat of earth, for I watch the waves with my outer rather than my inner eye. After all, the illusion is set off by an extraordinary, an almost miraculous thing—the embodiment of the wave beat in an almost constant shape. We see a wave a quarter of a mile off, then a few hundred yards nearer in, then just offshore; we seem to have been watching the same travelling mass of water—there has been no appreciable change in mass or in shape—yet all the while the original beat has taken on a flowing series of liquid bodies, bodies so alike, so much the same, that our eye will individualize them and follow them in—the third wave, we say, or the second wave behind the great wave. How strange it is that this beat of earth, this mysterious undulation of the seas, moving through and among the other forces stirring the waters close off the continent, should thus keep its constancy of form and mass, and how odd a blend of illusion and reality it all is! On the whole, the outer eye has the best of it.

Blowing all day long, a northwest wind yesterday swept the sky clear of every tatter and wisp of cloud. Clear it still is, though the wind has shifted to the east. The sky this afternoon is a harmony of universal blue, bordered with a surf rim of snowiest blue-white. Far out at sea, in the northeast and near the horizon, is a pool of the loveliest blue I have ever seen here—a light blue, a petal blue, blue of the emperor's gown in a Chinese fairy tale. If you would see waves at their best, come on such a day, when the ocean reflects a lovely sky, and the wind is light and onshore; plan to arrive in the afternoon so that you will have the sun facing the breakers. Come early, for the glints on the waves are most beautiful and interesting when the light is oblique and high. And come with a rising tide.

The surf is high, and on the far side of it, a wave greater than its fellows is shouldering out of the blue, glinting immensity of sea.

Friends tell me that there are certain tropic beaches where waves miles long break all at once in one cannonading crash: a little of this, I imagine, would be magnificent; a constancy of it, unbearable. The surf here is broken; it approaches the beach in long intercurrent parallels, some a few hundred feet long, some an eighth of a mile long, some, and the longest, attaining the quarter-mile length and perhaps just over. Thus, at all times and instants of the day, along the five miles of beach visible from the Fo'castle deck, waves are to be seen breaking, coursing in to break, seething up and sliding back.

But to return to the blue wave rolling in out of the blue spaciousness of sea. On the other side of the world, just opposite the Cape, lies the ancient Spanish province of Galicia, and the town of Pontevedra and St. James Compostella, renowned of pilgrims. (When I was there they offered me a silver cockle shell, but I would have none of it, and got myself a sea shell from some Galician fisherfolk.) Somewhere between this Spanish land and Cape Cod the pulse of earth has engendered this wave and sent it coursing westward through the seas. Far off the coast, the spray of its passing has, perhaps, risen on the windward bow of some rusty freighter and fallen in rainbow drops upon her plates; the great liners have felt it course beneath their keels.

A continent rises in the west, and the pulse beat approaches this bulwark of Cape Cod. Two thirds of a mile out, the wave is still a sea vibration, a billow. Slice it across, and its outline will be that of a slightly flattened semicircle; the pulse is shaped in a long, advancing mound. I watch it approach the beach. Closer and closer in, it is rising with the rise of the beach and the shoaling of the water; closer still, it is changing from a mound to a pyramid, a pyramid which swiftly distorts, the seaward side lengthening, the landward side incurving— the wave is now a breaker. Along the ridge of blue forms a rippling crest of clear, bright water; a little spray flies off. Under the racing foam churned up by the dissolution of other breakers the beach now catches at the last shape of sea inhabited by the pulse—the wave is *tripped* by the shoaling sand—the giant stumbles, crashes, and is pushed over and ahead by the sloping line of force behind. The fall of a breaker is never the work of gravity alone.

It is the last line of the wave that has captured the decorative imagination of the world—the long seaward slope, the curling crest, the incurved volute ahead.

Toppling over and hurled ahead, the wave crashes, its mass of glinting blue falling down in a confusion of seething, splendid white, the tumbling water rebounding from the sand to a height almost always a little above that of the original crest. Out of the wild, crumbling confusion born of the dissolution of the force and the last great shape, foamy fountains spurt, and ringlets of spray. The mass of water, still all furiously a-churn and seething white, now rushes for the rim of the beach as it might for an inconceivable cataract. Within thirty-five feet the water shoals from two feet to dry land. The edge of the rush thins, and the last impulse disappears in inch-deep slides of foam which reflect the sky in one last moment of energy and beauty and then vanish all at once into the sands.

Another thundering, and the water that has escaped and withdrawn is gathered up and swept forward again by another breaking wave. Night and day, age after age, so works the sea, with infinite variation obeying an unalterable rhythm moving through an intricacy of chance and law.

I can watch a fine surf for hours, taking pleasure in all its wild plays and variations. I like to stand on my beach, watching a long wave start breaking in many places, and see the curling water run north and south from the several beginnings, and collide in furious white pyramids built of the opposing energies. Splendid fountains often delight the eye. A towering and deep-bellied wave, toppling, encloses in its volute a quantity of air, and a few seconds after the spill this prisoned and compressed vapour bursts up through the boiling rush in feathery, foamy jets and geyser plumes. I have seen fountains here, on a September day, twenty and twenty-five and even thirty feet high. Sometimes a curious thing happens. Instead of escaping vertically, the rolled-up air escapes horizontally, and the breaker suddenly blows, as from a dragon's mouth, a great lateral puff of steamy spray. On sunny days, the toppling crest is often mirrored in the glassy volute as the wave is breaking. One lovely autumn afternoon, I saw a beautiful white gull sailing along the volute of a breaker accompanied by his reflection in the wave.

I add one curious effect of the wind. When the wind is directly offshore or well offshore, the waves approach fighting it; when the wind is offshore but so little off that its angle with the coast line is oblique—say an angle never greater than twenty-two degrees and never less than about twelve—the waves that approach the coast do not give battle, but run in with their long axis parallel to the wind. Sitting in the Fo'castle, I can often tell the exact quarter of an offshore wind simply by looking at this oblique alignment of the waves.

The long miles of beach are never more beautiful than when waves are rolling in fighting a strong breeze. Then do the breakers actually seem to charge the coast. As they approach, the wind meets them in a shock of war, the chargers rear but go on, and the wind blows back their manes. North and south, I watch them coursing in, the manes of white, sun brilliant spray streaming behind them for thirty and even forty feet. Sea horses do men call such waves on every coast of the world. If you would see them at their best, come to this beach on a bright October day when a northwest wind is billowing off to sea across the moors.

III

I will close my chapter with a few paragraphs about heavy surf.

It is best to be seen, I think, when the wind is not too high. A gale blows up a surf, but it also flattens out the incoming rollers, making monstrous, foamy travelling mounds of them much like those visible from a ship at sea. Not until the wind has dropped do the breakers gather form. The finest surf I have ever seen here—it was a Northern recoil of the great Florida hurricane—broke on three pleasant and almost windless autumn days. The storm itself had passed us, but our seas had been stirred to their deeps. Returning to the Cape at night from a trip to town, I heard the roar of the ocean in Orleans, and on arriving at Nauset, found the beach flooded to the dunes, and covered with a churn of surf and moonlight. Dragging a heavy suitcase and clad in my go-to-town clothes, I had an evil time getting to the Fo'castle over the dune tops and along the flooded marsh.

Many forces mingle in the surf of a storm— the great earth rhythm of the waves, the violence of wind, the struggle of water to obey its own elemental law. Out of the storm at sea come the giants and, being giants, trip far out, spilling first on the outer bar. Shoreward then they rush, breaking all the way. Touching the beach, they tumble in a roar lost in a general noise of storm. Trampled by the wind and everlastingly moved and lifted up and flung down by the incoming seas, the water offshore becomes a furious glassiness of marbly foam; wild, rushing sheets of seethe fifty feet wide border it; the water streams with sand.

Under all this move furious tidal currents, the longshore undertow of outer Cape Cod. Shore currents here move in a southerly direction; old wreckage and driftwood is forever being carried down here from the north. Coast guard friends often look at a box or stick I have retrieved, and say, "Saw that two weeks ago up by the light."

After an easterly, I find things on the beach which have been blown down from the Gulf of Maine—young, uprooted spruce trees, lobster buoys from Matinicus, and, after one storm, a great strewing of empty sea-urchin shells. Another easterly washed up a strewing of curious wooden pebbles shaped by the sea out of the ancient submerged forests which lie just off the present coast. They were brown-black, shaped like beach stones, and as smooth as such stones.

The last creature I found in the surf was a huge horseshoe crab, the only one I have ever chanced to find on the outside. Poor *Limulus polyphemus!* The surf having turned him upside down, he had as usual doubled up, and the surf had then filled with sand the angle of his doubling. When I discovered him, he was being bullied by a foam slide, and altogether in a desperate way. So I picked him up, rinsed the sand out of his waving gills, held him up all dripping by the tail, and flung him as far as I could to seaward of the breakers. A tiny splash, and I had seen the last of him, a moment more, and the surf had filled the hollow in which he had lain.

Autumnal easterlies and November tides having scoured from the beach its summer deeps of sand, the high seasonal tides now run clear across to the very foot of the dunes. Under this daily overflow of cold, the last of the tide-rim hoppers and foragers vanish from the beach. An icy wind blusters; I hear a dry tinkle of sand against my western wall; December nears, and winter closes in upon the coast.

Chapter IV

MIDWINTER

I

A year indoors is a journey along a paper calendar; a year in outer nature is the accomplishment of a tremendous ritual. To share in it, one must have a knowledge of the pilgrimages of the sun, and something of that natural sense of him and feeling for him which made even the most primitive people mark the summer limits of his advance and the last December ebb of his decline. All these autumn weeks I have watched the great disk going south along the horizon of moorlands beyond the marsh, now sinking behind this field, now behind this leafless tree, now behind this sedgy hillock dappled with thin snow. We lose a great deal, I think, when we lose this sense and feeling for the sun. When all has been said, the adventure of the sun is the great natural drama by which we live, and not to have joy in it and awe of it, not to share in it, is to close a dull door on nature's sustaining and poetic spirit.

The splendour of colour in this world of sea and dune ebbed from it like a tide; it shallowed first without seeming to lose ground, and presently vanished all at once, almost, so it seemed, in one grey week. Warmth left the sea, and winter came down with storms of rushing wind and icy, pelting rain. The first snow fell early in November, just before the dawn of a grey and bitter day. I had written a letter the night before, intending to give it to the coast guardsman who came south at seven o'clock, but somehow or other I missed him; and no welcome light flashed an answer to mine as I stood on the crest of my dune looking into the darkness of the beach and listening to the sombre thunder of a rising sea. Unwilling to stay up till after midnight for the next patrol, I went out and put a note on the coast guard key post just south of me asking the last man south in the morning to wake me up and come in and get the letter. At about half-past five I woke to a stamping of feet and a knock on the door, and in came John Blood, the tall, light-haired New Yorker, very much buttoned up into his blue pea jacket, and with his watch cap well pulled down upon his ears.

"Ahoy, John—thanks for coming in. What's it like outside?"

"It's snowing. Winter's come, I guess," he said, with a meditative grin.

We talked, I gave him the letter, and he went out into the dark break of dawn, the wind, and the snow.

My fire had gone out, the Fo'castle was raw and cold, but my wood was ready, and I soon had a fire crackling. All winter long, I kept a basket of little sticks and fragments of driftwood ready for the morning, and began the day with a bonfire in the fireplace. A hearthful of high, leaping flame sends out a quick and plentiful heat. Light came slowly into the world, coming not so much from the east as from some vague, general nowhere—a light that did not grow brighter but only increased in quantity. A northwest snow squall was blowing across the sedgy marshes and the dunes, "seeming nowhere to alight" in the enormous landscape, and whirling off to the sullen, iron-green, and icy sea. As I watched, half-a-dozen gulls came sailing over from the marsh. These birds like foul weather and have a way of flying out over along the breakers a few minutes after the edge of a cloud has hidden the sun, and there is a strange, ominous sense of storm in this great natural scene.

The snow skirred along the beach, the wind suffering it no rest; I saw little whirlpools of it driving down the sand into the onrush of the breakers, it gathered in the footprints of the coast guard patrols, building up on their leeward side and patterning them in white on the empty beach. The very snow in the air had a character of its own, for it was the snow of the outer Cape and the North Atlantic, snow icy and crystalline, and sweeping across the dunes and moors rather than down upon them. Chancing to look to the north, I saw Nauset Light still turning and gleaming, and as I watched, it suddenly sank to a storm-smothered and distant glow and stopped. By the almanac, the sun had risen. So began the worst winter on the Cape for close upon fifty years, a winter marked by great storms and tides, six wrecks, and the loss of many lives.

The sun, this December morning, has come to the end of his southern journey, he climbs the whitish sky to the south over the white fury

of the Orleans shoals, and takes on a silvery
quality from the pallor of the sky. On such a
morning went ancient peoples to their hills,
and cried to the pale god to return to their
woods and fields; perhaps the vanished Nausets
danced a ceremonial dance on those inland
moors, and the same northwest wind carried the
measured drumming to these dunes. A morning
to go out upon the dunes and study the work of
winter. Between the cold blue of the sea and
the levels of the marshes, the long wall of the
dunes lies blanched to a whiter pallor than the
surrounding landscape, for there is no russet and
but little gold in dune grass when it dies. That
intricacy of green, full-fleshed life, which billowed
like wild wheat in the summer's southwest wind,
has thinned away now to a sparse world of
separate heads, each one holding, as in a fist, a
clump of whitish and mildewed wires.

The sand moves beneath. This shrinking of
summer's vegetation, this uncovering of the
body of the dune, has permitted the winter gales
to reach the sand, and all up and down the great
wall, on the tops of the dunes, the surface sand is
moving. The direction of this movement varies,
of course, with the direction of the wind, but in

general the movement is toward the sea, for the prevailing winter winds are northwesterly. In some places the blown and creeping sand has covered the grass so deeply that only the very tips of the withered spikes rise out of it; in other places, on the landward rims of the dunes, the wind has blown the sand entirely away from the plant and left a withered tangle of roots and stalks sprawling in the wind. Here and there, in the dead, whitish grass, one encounters a stray tiny spotlet of snow, relic of a storm a fortnight past. Such spots linger here for inexplicable weeks and have an air of things disregarded and forgotten.

I have written of the movement of sand on the surface of the dune, yet the very essence of the work of winter here is the quieting, the enchainment of the mass of the sand. The sun no longer being hot enough to dry it, moisture lies on it and within it, it loses its fluidity, it takes on weight and definition. Footprints which the summer would erase in a quarter of an hour remain in well-sheltered places for days and even weeks. There is a winter change of colour, as well. The warm golden quality vanishes and is replaced by a tone of cold silver-grey, which makes no flashing answer to the sun.

Animal life has disappeared into the chill air, the heavy, lifeless sand. On the surface, nothing remains of the insect world. That multiplicity of insect tracks, those fantastic ribbons which grasshoppers, promenading flies, spiders, and beetles printed on the dunes as they went about their hungry and mysterious purposes, have come to an end in this world and left it all the poorer. Those trillions of unaccountable lives, those crawling, buzzing, intense presences which nature created to fulfil some unknown purpose or perhaps simply to satisfy a whim for a certain sound or a moment of exquisite colour, where are they now, in this vast world, silent save for the sombre thunder of the surf and the rumble of wind in the porches of the ears? As I muse here, it occurs to me that we are not sufficiently grateful for the great symphony of natural sound which insects add to the natural scene; indeed, we take it so much as a matter of course that it does not stir our fully conscious attention. But all those little fiddles in the grass, all those cricket pipes, those delicate flutes, are they not lovely beyond words when heard in midsummer on a moonlight night? I like, too, the movement they give to a landscape with their rushes, their

strange comings and goings, and their hoverings
with the sun's brilliance reflected in their wings.
Here, and at this especial moment, there is no
trace or vestige of the summer's insect world,
yet one feels them here, the trillion, trillion tiny
eggs in grass and marsh and sand, all faithfully
spun from the vibrant flesh of innumerable
mothers, all faithfully sealed and hidden away,
all waiting for the rush of this earth through
space and the resurgence of the sun.

I find no more paths of little paws and claw-
tipped feet, each one with its own rhythm, its
own mechanics of walking and running. The
skunks, who linger till the last chilled grasshopper has been pounced on and eaten, are now
lying torpid in their dark snuggles underground,
their heartbeat stilled to a ghost of its summer
self. They do not, apparently, make themselves
burrows on the dunes, perhaps because a wise
instinct warns them that a burrow in these open
sands might collapse about them as they slept.
November finds them travelling up the dunes to
the firm soil of the mainland moors. The hill
nearest the dunes is full of their winter parlours.
Twice during the winter I saw a wildcat of
domestic stock hunting along the edge of the

marsh, and marked how savagery had completely altered the creature's gait, for it slunk along, belly close to the grass, like a panther. A large brown cat with long fur and a wild and extraordinarily foolish face. I imagined it was out hunting the marsh larks who feed in the stubble of the salt-hay fields. Another time, I saw the hoofs of a deer in the sand, but of this deer and its adventures in the frozen marsh I shall speak later.

At Orleans, an otter, a rare animal here, has been seen, the man who saw it taking it for a seal until it came out of the breakers and ran along the sand. Every now and then, from the windows of the Fo'castle, I catch sight of a seal's black head swimming about close inshore. In summer, seals are rarely seen on this part of the great outer beach—I myself have never seen one—but in winter they come along the breakers reconnoitring in search of food. They have a trick of swimming unperceived under a flock of sea ducks, seizing one of the unwary birds from underneath, and then disappearing with their mouths full of flesh and frantic feathers. A confusion follows; the survivors leap from the water with wildly beating wings, they scatter, wheel, and gather again, and presently nature has erased every sign of the struggle, and the sea rolls on as before.

There has been a strange tragedy to the north; one of those dread elemental things that happen in an elemental world. The other evening my friend Bill Eldredge, of Nauset, told me that there had been a disaster that same morning off the Race. Two fishermen who had left Provincetown in a big, thirty-foot motor dory were seen from the beach to be having trouble of some kind; the dory had then drifted into a tide rip churned up with surf, and capsized and drowned her crew. A few nights later, Bill came south again, and I stood for a moment talking to him on the beach at the foot of the Fo'castle dune. A lovely night of great winter stars and a quiet sea. "You remember those two fishermen I was telling you about?" said Bill. "They've found them both now. One of them had a son at Wood End Station, and when he was coming back from his patrol last night he saw his father's body on the beach."

II

On the night of Saturday, January 1st, it was almost pitch dark along the coast. In the murk,

the eye of Nauset Light had a reddish tinge, and,
turning, revealed a world shaped like a disk and
pressed between a great darkness of earth and
a low, black floor of cloud. The wind was on
shore and blowing strong. Some time after
midnight, a surfman from Cahoons Hollow
Coast Guard Station, patrolling south, discovered a schooner in the surf, with the seas
breaking over her, and the crew hollering in the
rigging. I write "hollering" here without shame,
for "hallooing," or whatever the proper spelling
of the verb may be, simply would not tell the
story, or convey the sound heard in the
night. After holding up a red signal flare to tell
the men on the wreck that they had been seen,
the surfman hurried on to Cahoons and gave
the alarm. The crew of the station, under
command of Captain Henry Daniels, then
dragged their cart of life-saving apparatus down
the beach through a surf running to the bank,
and took off every single man safely in the
breeches buoy. The prompt and gallant rescue
had been no easy task, with the tide thus running high and the seas breaking over the
schooner.

I had my first view of her the next afternoon.

She turned out to be the two-masted, motor-auxiliary fishing schooner *A. Roger Hickey*, Boston-bound from the fishing grounds. Her compass had been at fault, they said. When I caught sight of her from the top of a path descending the great earth cliff of the Cape, the vessel lay on the open sand a mile up the beach to the north, a typical Boston fisherman with a red bottom and a black hull. A vessel, I judged, something over a hundred feet long. The whole vast view was really a picture of singular and moving beauty; it would be hard to forget, I think, that immense and jade-green ocean under a fine sky, the great, sepia-brown beach with its overhanging haze of faintest violet, the bright ship so forlorn, and the tiny black figures moving round and about it. The beach had already begun to break up its prize. Along it, on my way to the ship, I saw splintered wood, an undamaged hatch cover painted white, and several bunches of water-logged manila tags with a fish merchant's name printed on them in large black letters.

Presently there came walking toward me three ladies of Wellfleet, good, pleasant New England housewives, each one with a large haddock under her arm rolled up in a sheet of newspaper, the three dead-eyed haddock heads protruding as from paper collars, the three fish tails visible behind. Apparently the fish which the *Hickey* had on board when she struck were being given away.

Arriving at the wreck, I found that her rudder had already carried away, and that her timbers were badly wrenched, and her seams opened. The ship's dog, who had been thrillingly rescued in his master's arms, sat shivering on the beach, a most inoffensive and unromantic brown dog with what looked like an appalling case of mange. A handful of visitors, men and boys in workaday clothes and rubber boots, were wandering round the vessel, their boot prints making a chain about her on the beach, and other men were busy puttering round the steeply tilted deck. Finding Captain Henry Daniels of Cahoons aboard, an old friend of years' standing, I heard that the crew of the *Hickey*, two or three excepted, had already returned to Boston by train, and that the vessel was so badly damaged that she was to be stripped as soon as possible of all gear worth saving, and abandoned.

Midships, a discussion was going on round

the open mouth of one of the fish holds. The *Hickey's* catch was still there, a mass of big greyish fish bodies, haddocks with staring eyes, cod with chin whiskers, flounders, and huge lemon soles. The discussion concerned the possibility of the fish having had a bath in fuel oil when the seas washed into the *Hickey* at high tide. No one took serious alarm, and the fish, handed out to all comers by a member of the crew, proved excellent eating.

So they stripped the *A. Roger Hickey*, took out her engine and such gear as they could, and then someone set fire to the hulk. By the end of the winter, there was not even a splinter of this vessel on the beach. She was the third wreck, and there were others to come.

As the winter closed in upon the beach, I began to look forward to days when I might see what took place there during icy weather, but such opportunities proved even rarer than I had expected. Thrust forth as it is into the outer Atlantic, the Cape has a climate of island quality and island moderation. Low temperatures may occur, but the thermometer almost never falls as low as it does on the inner Massachusetts coast, nor do "spells" of cold weather "hang on" for any length of time. Storms which are snowstorms on the continental mainland turn to rainstorms on the Cape, and such snowstorms as do arrive form but a crust upon these Eastham moors. Two days after the storm the snow has thinned to great decorative patches on the slopes of sedgy hills; in another day only fragments, drifts, and stray islets remain. There is even a difference of temperature between the mainland moors of Eastham and the dunes. It is warmer on the bar. On a casual winter day I have noted a difference of eight degrees.

The work of cold weather—I mean weather when the temperature sinks toward zero—is thus to be observed only on occasion along this beach. When it comes, it comes all at once, creates a new world overnight, and vanishes overnight. The agency that brings it is the northwest wind sweeping down on us across Massachusetts Bay from the forests and frozen lakes of northern Canada. I remember one of the nights of its coming, a Thursday night early in January with great winter clouds moving out to sea, opening and closing over the cold stars, the wind on the beach so icy that I found myself, when I first went out into it, breathing

it in little reluctant breaths. The next day was
as cold and desolate a day as I have ever seen
upon the beach. The ocean was purple-black,
rough, and covered with sombre whitecaps; the
morning light was pewter dull, and over earth
and sea and the lonely sands hung a pall of
purple-leaden cloud full of vast, tormented motion as it crossed the Cape on its way to the
Atlantic. Looking off to sea, as I walked down
my dune to go exploring, I saw a solitary
freighter hugging the coast for shelter from the
northwest wind; she was plunging heavily in
the great seas and flinging up tons of spray with
each plunge, and her bow and her forward deck
were already thick with ice. Gulls flew along
the iron-black and sombre breakers of the ebb,
their white plumage chalky in that impure and
arctic light. The wind was a thing to search the
marrow of one's bones.

Two beaches had formed in the icy night, best
seen and studied at low tide. The upper beach
occupied the width between the dunes and the
line of the night's high tide; the lower beach
sloped from this high-tide mark to the open sea.
The upper beach and the dunes were frozen
hard. The frozen sand was delightful to walk

upon, for the tiny congealed grains afforded a safe, sustaining footing, and the surface, though solid, had the resiliency of thick, unvarnished linoleum on a good floor. It was an odd, an unnatural experience, to hit one's foot on a ridge of frozen sand. Fragments of wreckage imbedded in the sand, wreaths of imbedded seaweed—all these were as immovable as so many rocks. At the very foot of the largest of the dunes, I found a male surf scoter or skunk coot frozen stiff. A few solid kicks dislodged it, and I picked it up, but could find no wound. The lower beach, that is to say the width that had been covered by the tide during the night, was frozen solid at its junction with the upper beach, but the fine slope down to the breakers, though frozen firm, was not frozen through and through. Along the edge of the breakers, it was not frozen at all.

Between these two beaches, one above, one below, one frozen solid, the other crusted over, there ran a kind of frontier some eight or ten feet wide, a no-man's-land of conflicting natural forces. At the height of the night tide, the seething foam rims of the sliding surf, flung by the ocean into the face of the night cold, had frozen on the sloping beach in layers of salt ice which preserved all the curves and foamy ridges of the captured edge of the sea. The brim of a high tide, that very spirit of energy and motion, lay there motionless on a beach itself deprived of motion; the scalloped edges, the little curls of foam, the long, reaching, rushing tongues, all these were to be seen enchanted into that ocean ice which is so much like a kind of snow. At its upper edge this image of the surf brim was but a glaze of ice on the beach; at its lower edge it was twelve to fifteen inches in height and fell off sheer, like an ice cake, to the beach below. And north and south it ran, mile upon icy mile, as far as the eye could see.

The subsequent history of this ice is not without interest. After two days of bitter cold the wind changed in the night, and that night's tide quietly removed every vestige of the ice cakes from the beach. The swathe on which the ice had lain, however, remained half visible, for there water and sand had mingled and frozen deep. Presently the upper beach thawed, the cold crumbling drily out of the sand, and the lower beach, which had yielded its frozen surface to each succeeding tide and frozen again during the ebb, remained as the last tide left it. Between the two beaches, the width of buried ice lingered for a fortnight, resisting sun and whole days of winter rain. It had a way of coming suddenly to an end, and of beginning as suddenly again; sand drifted over it, the tide edge seeped through to it, the moving beach, forever adjusting itself to complex forces, burst it open, yet it lingered on. For all of us who used the beach, this buried width of ice became a secret road. The coast guards knew it well and followed along it in the night. As I set down these words, I think of the times I have come to a blind end and prodded the sand with my beach staff in search of that secret footing. Little by little the sun and the tides wore down its resistance, and so it disappeared, and our searching feet knew it no more.

The great marsh was another desolation on that same overcast and icy day. Salt ice had formed in wide rims along the edges of the great level islands, the shallower channels had frozen over, and the deeper ones were strewn with ice cakes sailing and turning about in the currents of the tides. The scene had taken on a certain winter unity, for the ice had bound the channels and the islands together into one wide and wintry plain.

On the next morning—it was sunny then, but still freezing cold—I chanced to go out for a moment to look at the marsh. About a mile and a half away, in one of the open channels, was a dark something which looked like a large, unfamiliar bird. A stray goose, perhaps? Taking my glass, I found the dark object to be the head of a deer swimming down the channel, and, even as I looked, there came to my ears the distant barking of dogs. A pair of marauding curs, out hunting on their own, had found a deer somewhere and driven the creature down the dunes and into the icy creeks. Down the channel it swam, and presently turned aside and climbed out on the marsh island just behind the Fo'castle. The animal was a young doe. I thought then, and I still believe, that this doe and the unseen creature whose delicate hoofprints I often found near the Fo'castle were one and the same. It lived, I believe, in the pines on the northern shore of the marsh and came down to the dunes at earliest dawn. But to return to its adventures: All afternoon I watched it standing on the island far out in the marsh, the tall, dead sea grass rising about its russet body; when night came, it was still there, a tiny spot of forlorn mammalian life in that

frozen scene. Was it too terrified to return?
That night a tide of unusual height was due
which would submerge the islands under at
least two feet of water and floating ice. Would
the doe swim ashore under cover of darkness?
I went out at midnight into my solitary world
and saw the ice-covered marsh gleaming palely
under a sky of brilliant stars, but could see
nothing of the island of the doe save a ghostliness
of salt ice along the nearer rim.

The first thing I did, on waking the next
morning, was to search the island with my
glass. The doe was still there.

I have often paused to wonder how that
delicate and lovely creature endured so cruel a
night, how she survived the slow rise of the icy
tide about her poor legs, and the northwest gale
that blustered about her all night long in that
starlit loneliness of crunchy marsh mud and
the murmur of the tides. The morning lengthened, the sun rose higher on the marsh, and
presently the tide began to rise again. I watched
it rising toward the refugee, and wondered if
she could survive a second immersion. Just a
little before noon, perhaps as the water was
flooding round her feet, she came down to the

edge of her island, and plunged into the channel. The creek was full of ice mush and of ice floes moving at a good speed; the doe was weak, the ice cakes bore down upon her, striking her heavily; she seemed confused, hesitated, swam here, swam there, stood still, and was struck cruelly by a floe which seemed to pass over her, yet on she swam, bewildered, but resolute for life. I had almost given up hope for her, when rescue came unexpectedly. My friend Bill Eldredge, it appeared, while on watch in the station tower the day before had chanced to see the beginning of the story, and on the second morning had noticed the doe still standing in the marshes. All the Nauset crew had taken an interest. Catching sight of the poor creature fighting for life in the drift, three of the men put off in a skiff, poled the ice away with their oars, and shepherded the doe ashore. "When she reached dry land, she couldn't rise, she was so weak, and fell down again and again. But finally she stood up and stayed up, and walked off into the pines."

III

I have now to tell of the great northeast storm of February 19th and 20th. They say here that it was the worst gale known on the outer Cape since the *Portland* went down with all hands on that terrible November night in '98.

It began after midnight on a Friday night, and the barometer gave but little warning of its coming. That Friday afternoon I had walked up the beach to Nauset Station, found Bill Eldredge on watch in the tower, and asked him to wake me up when he went by at midnight. "Never mind if you don't see a light," I said. "Come in anyway and wake me up. I may go down the beach with you." I often made the patrols with the men at the station, for I liked to walk the beach by night.

Shortly after midnight, Bill came to the door, but I did not get up and dress to go down the beach with him, for I was rather tired from piling up a mass of driftwood, so I sat up in bed and talked to him by the dying light of my fire. On bitter nights, I used to put a big log on in the hope that it might flicker and smoulder till morning, but on average nights, I let the fire die down to a bed of ashes, for I am a light sleeper, and the little play of flames on the hearth kept me awake. Living in outer nature keeps the senses keen, and living alone stirs in them a certain watchfulness.

The coast guardsman stood against the brick fireplace, his elbow propped for a moment on the shelf; I scarce could see his blue-clad figure in the gloom. "It's blowing up," he said. "I think we are going to have a northeaster." I apologized for not getting up, pleaded weariness, and, after a little talk, Bill said that he must be going, and returned to the beach. I saw him use his flashlight a moment as he plunged down the dune.

I woke in the morning to the dry rattle of sleet on my eastern windows and the howling of wind. A northeaster laden with sleet was bearing down on the Cape from off a furious ocean, an ebbing sea fought with a gale blowing directly on the coast; the lonely desolation of the beach was a thousand times more desolate in that white storm pouring down from a dark sky. The sleet fell as a heavy rain falls when it is blown about by the wind. I built up my fire, dressed, and went out, shielding my face from the sleet by pulling my head down into the collar of my coat. I brought in basket after basket of firewood, till the corner of the room resembled a woodshed. Then I folded up the bedclothes, threw my New Mexican blanket over the couch, lighted the oil stove, and prepared breakfast. An apple, oatmeal porridge, toast made at the fireplace, a boiled egg, and coffee.

Sleet and more of it, rushes of it, attacks of it, screaming descents of it; I heard it on the roof, on the sides of the house, on the windowpanes. Within, my fire fought against the cold, tormented light. I wondered about a small fishing boat, a thirty-foot "flounder dragger" that had anchored two miles or so off the Fo'castle the evening before. I looked for her with my glass, but could not see into the storm.

Streaming over the dunes, the storm howled on west over the moors. The islands of the marsh were brownish black, the channels leaden and whipped up by the wind; and along the shores of the desolate islands, channel waves broke angrily, chidingly, tossing up heavy ringlets of lifeless white. A scene of incredible desolation and cold. All day long I kept to my house, building up the fire and keeping watch from the windows; now and then I went out to see that all was well with the Fo'castle and its foundations, and to glimpse what I could, through the sleet, of the storm on the sea. For a mile or so offshore the North Atlantic was a convulsion of elemental fury whipped by the sleety wind, the great parallels of the breakers tumbling all together and mingling in one seething and immense confusion, the sound of this mile of surf being an endless booming roar, a seethe, and a dread grinding, all intertwined with the high scream of the wind. The rush of the inmost breakers up the beach was a thing of violence and blind will. Darkness coming early, I closed my shutters on the uproar of the outer world, all save one shutter on the landward side.

With the coming of night the storm increased; the wind reaching a velocity of seventy to eighty miles an hour. It was at this time, I am told, that friends on the mainland began to be worried about me, many of them looking for my light. My lamp, a simple kerosene affair with a white china shade, stood on a table before the unshuttered window facing the land. An old friend said he would see it or think that he saw it for a half minute or so, and then it would vanish for hours into the darkness of the gale. It was singularly peaceful in the little house. Presently, the tide, which had ebbed a little during the afternoon, turned and began to come in. All afternoon long the surf had thundered high upon the beach, the ebb tide backed up against the wind. With the turn of the tide came fury unbelievable. The great rhythm of its waters now at one with the rhythm of the wind, the ocean rose out of the night to attack the ancient rivalry of earth, hurling breaker after thundering breaker against the long bulwark of the sands. The Fo'castle, being low and strongly built, stood solid as a rock, but its walls thrummed in the gale. I could feel the vibration in the bricks of the chimney, and the dune beneath the house trembled incessantly with the onslaught of the surf.

Where were my friends at Nauset Station, thought I, in this furious night. Who was on his way north, with seven miles of night and sleet to battle through before he returned to the shelter of the station and the warmth of that kitchen stove which is kept polished to a brilliance beyond all stoves? It was Bill, as a matter of fact, and because of the surf on the beach he was using the path which runs along the top of the cliff close by its brim, a path exposed to the full violence of the gale. As I mused thus, troubled about my friends, there came a knock at my open window, and then steps outside and a knock at the door. Letting my visitor in was easy enough, but to close the door after him was another matter. Closing the door against the force of the gale was like trying to close it upon something material; it was exactly as if I were pressing the door against a bulging mass of felt. My visitor was Albert Robbins, first man south from Nauset, a big powerful youngster and a fine lad; he was covered with sleet and sand, sand and sleet in his hair, in his eyebrows, in the corners of his eyes, in his ears, behind his ears, in the corners of his mouth, in his nostrils even. And a cheerful, determined grin!

"Wanted to see if you were still here," he said humorously, rooting sand out of his eyes with a knuckle. I busied myself getting him a cup of steaming coffee.

"Any news? Anyone in trouble?" I asked.

"Yes, there's a coast guard patrol boat off the Highland; something's the matter with her engine. She's anchored off there, and they've sent two destroyers out from Boston to get her."

"When did you hear that?"

"This afternoon."

"Didn't hear anything else?"

"No, the wires blew down, and we can't get beyond Cahoons."

"Think they've got any chance if the destroyers haven't got to them?"

"Gosh, I hope so," he said; and then, after a pause, "but it don't look like it." And then, "So long," and into the storm again.

I did not go to bed, for I wanted to be ready for any eventuality. As the hour of flood tide neared, I dressed as warmly as I could, turned down my lamp, and went out upon the dunes.

An invisible moon, two days past the full, had risen behind the rushing floor of cloud, and some of its wan light fell on the tortured earth and the torment of the sea. The air was full of sleet, hissing with a strange, terrible, insistent sound on the dead grass, and sand was being whirled up into the air. Being struck on the face by this sand and sleet was like being lashed by a tiny, pin-point whip. I have never looked on such a tide. It had crossed the beach, climbed the five-foot wall of the dune levels that run between the great mounds, and was hurling wreckage fifty and sixty feet into the starved white beach grass; the marsh was an immense flooded bay, and the "cuts" between the dunes and the marsh rivers of breakers. A hundred yards to the north of me was such a river; to the south, the surf was attempting to flank the dune, an attempt which did not succeed. Between these two onslaughts, no longer looking *down* upon the sea, but directly into it and just over it, the Fo'castle stood like a house built out into the surf on a mound of sand. A third of a mile or so to the north I chanced to see rather a strange thing. The dune bank there was washing away and caving in under the onslaught of the seas, and presently there crumbled out the blackened skeleton of an ancient wreck which the dunes had buried long ago. As the tide rose this ghost floated and lifted itself free, and then washed south close along the dunes. There was something inconceivably spectral in the sight of this dead hulk thus stirring from its grave and yielding its bones again to the fury of the gale.

As I walked in the night I wondered about the birds who live here in the marsh. That great population of gulls, ducks, and geese and their rivals and allies—where were they all crouching, where were they hidden in that wild hour?

All Sunday morning there was sleet—more sleet fell in this storm than the Cape had seen in a generation—-and then, about the middle of the afternoon, the wind died down, leaving a wild sea behind. Going to Nauset Station, I had news of the disaster at the Highland. The destroyers, in spite of a splendid battle, had been unable to reach the disabled patrol boat, and the luckless ship had gone to pieces. It is thought that she dragged onto the outer bar. Nine men had perished. Two bodies came ashore next day; their watches had stopped at five o'clock, so we knew that the vessel had weathered the night and gone to pieces in the morning. What a night they must have had, poor souls!

There was wreckage everywhere, great logs, tree stumps, fragments of ships, planking, splintered beams, boards, rough timber, and, by itself in the surf, the enormous rudder of the *Hickey*, splintered sternpost and all. The day after the storm, people came down from Eastham in farm wagons and Fords, looked at the sea for a while, talked over the storm with whoever happened to be standing by, paid a call on the coast guards, and then went casually to work piling up the best of the timber. I saw Bill Eldredge in one of the cuts sorting out planks to be used in building a henhouse. Gulls were milling over the surf and spume—the greatest numbers gathering where the surf was most discoloured—and gulls were flying back and forth between the breakers and the marsh. From their point of view, perhaps, nothing had happened.

Chapter V

WINTER VISITORS

I

During the winter the world of the dunes and the great beach was entirely my own, and I lived at the Fo'castle as undisturbed as Crusoe on his island. Man disappeared from the world of nature in which I lived almost as if he, too, were a kind of migratory bird. It is true that I could see the houses of Eastham village on the uplands across the marsh, and the passing ships and fishing boats, but these were the works of man rather than man himself. By the middle of February the sight of an unknown someone walking on the beach near the Fo'castle would have been a historical event. Should any ask how I endured this isolation in so wild a place and in the depth of winter, I can only answer that I enjoyed every moment to the full. To be able to see and study undisturbed the processes of nature—I like better the old Biblical phrase "mighty works"—

is an opportunity for which any man might well feel reverent gratitude, and here at last, in this silence and isolation of winter, a whole region was mine whose innermost natural life might shape itself to its ancient courses without the hindrance and interferences of man. No one came to kill, no one came to explore, no one even came to see. Earth, ocean, and sky, the triune unity of this coast, pursued each one their vast and mingled purposes as untroubled by man as a planet on its course about the sun.

It is not good to be too much alone, even as it is unwise to be always with and in a crowd, but, solitary as I was, I had few opportunities for moods or to "lose and neglect the creeping hours of time." From the moment that I rose in the morning and threw open my door looking toward the sea to the moment when the spurt of a match sounded in the evening quiet of my solitary house, there was always something to do, something to observe, something to record, something to study, something to put aside in a corner of the mind. There was the ocean in all weathers and at all tides, now grey and lonely and veiled in winter rain, now sun-bright, coldly green, and marbled with dissolving foam; there was the marsh with its great congresses, its little companies, its wandering groups, and little family gatherings of winter birds; there was the glory of the winter sky rolling out of the ocean over and across the dunes, constellation by constellation, lonely star by star. To see the night sky in all its divinity of beauty, the world beneath it should be lovely, too, else the great picture is split in halves which no mind can ever really weld into a unity of reverence. I think the nights on which I felt most alone (if I paused to indulge myself in such an emotion) were the nights when southeasterly rains were at work in the dark, immense world outside my door dissolving in rain and fog such ice and snow as lingered on after a snowfall or a cold spell had become history. On such southeasterly nights, the fog lay thick on marsh and ocean, the distant lights of Eastham vanished in a universal dark, and on the invisible beach below the dune, great breakers born of fog swell and the wind rolled up the sands with the slow, mournful pace of stately victims destined to immolation, and toppled over, each one, in a heavy, awesome roar that faded to silence before a fellow victim followed on out of the darkness on the sea. Only one sense impression lingered to remind me of the vanished world of man, and that the long, long complaints and melancholy bellowings of vessels feeling their way about miles offshore.

But I was not entirely alone. My friends the coast guards at Nauset Station, patrolling the beach every night and in all weathers, often came in to see how I was faring, to hand me on a letter, or to tell me the news of the Cape. My pleasure in such visits was very real, and between half after seven and eight o'clock I always hoped for a step. When one has not spoken to another human being for twenty-four hours, a little conversation is pleasant exercise, though to the speaker the simplest phrases, even the simple idiom, "Come in," may take on a quaint air of being breathless and voluble. Sometimes no one came, and I spent the evening by my fire reading quietly, going over my notes, and wondering who it was who walked the beach.

It is not easy to live alone, for man is a gregarious creature; especially in his youth, powerful instincts offer battle to such a way of life, and in utter solitude odd things may happen to the mind. I lived as a solitary, yes, but I made no pretence of acting the conventional hermit of the pious tract and the Eighteenth Century romance. With my weekly trips to Orleans to buy fresh bread and butter, my frequent visits to the Overlook, and my conversations with the men on night patrol, a mediæval anchorite would have probably regarded me as a dweller in the market place. It was not this touch with my fellows, however, which alone sustained me. Dwelling thus upon the dunes, I lived in the midst of an abundance of natural life which manifested itself every hour of the day, and from being thus surrounded, thus enclosed within a great whirl of what one may call the life force, I felt that I drew a secret and sustaining energy. There were times, on the threshold of spring, when the force seemed as real as heat from the sun. A sceptic may smile and ask me to come to his laboratory and demonstrate; he may talk as he will of the secret workings of my own isolated and uninfluenced flesh and blood, but I think that those who have lived in nature, and tried to open their doors rather than close them on her energies, will understand well enough what I mean. Life is as much a force in the universe as electricity or gravitational pull, and the presence of life sustains life. Individuals may destroy individuals, but the life force may mingle with the individual life as a billow of fire may mingle for a moment with a candle flame.

But now I must begin to tell of the birds who are wintering on the coast, of the exchange of species which takes place here, and of how all manage to live.

As I walk the beach on a bright and blustery January morning, my first impression is one of space, beauty, and loneliness. The summer bird life of the beach has completely disappeared, and at the moment of which I tell, not a single beach bird or sea bird, not even a resident gull, is to be seen on the beach along all these empty miles. I walk, and no terns come swooping down at me out of the dunes, scolding me for my intrusion on their immense and ancient privacy; no sandpipers rise at my approach, wheel over the inner breakers, and settle down again a hundred yards ahead. Summer residents and autumn migrants of the beach, sandpipers, plovers, yellow-legs, "knots," and sanderlings, all have gone south with the sun and are now to be found anywhere from the Carolinas south to Patagonia. The familiar sanderlings—it is of *Crocethia alba* that I write—lingered surprisingly late; they seemed almost as numerous in October as in August, there were plenty to be seen in November, but in December flocks were rare, and by Christmas, there were only a few strays and cripples left behind.

New Year's Day, on the deserted beach, I surprised a little flock of ruddy turnstones, *Arenaria interpres morinella*, who took wing on my approach and flew south close along the seaward face of the dunes. I shall always remember this picture as one of the most beautiful touches of colour I have ever seen in nature, for the three dominant colours of this bird—who is a little larger than the semipalmated sandpiper—are black, white, and glowing chestnut red; and these colours are interestingly displayed in patches and bold stripes seen at their best when the bird is flying. The great dunes behind them and the long vista of the beach were cold silver overlaid with that faint, loveliest violet which is the overtone colour of the coast.

As I watched these decorative birds flying away ahead of me into that vast ocean world, I began thinking of how little has ever been written or said about the loveliness of our North Atlantic birds. There are plenty of books about

them, there are a world of kind people who
cherish and love them as birds, but there is a
lack of printed material and discussion cele-
brating their qualities of beauty. Such æsthetic
appreciation of our shore birds as we have had
seems to have reached that showy and unfortunate creature, the wood duck, *Aix sponsa*,
and been permanently overcome. Now, the
turnstone is a lovely little bird, the least tern is
another; the king eider is a magnificent creature,
and there are many more whose beauty deserves
comment and attention. A second notion, too,
came into my head as I saw the turnstones fly
away—that no one really knows a bird until he
has seen it in flight. Since my year upon the
dunes, spent in a world of magnificent fliers, I
have been tempted to believe that the relation
of the living bird with its wings folded to the
living bird in flight is almost that of the living
bird to the same bird stuffed. In certain cases,
the difference between the bird on the wing and
the bird at rest is so great that one might be
watching two different creatures. Not only do
colours and new arrangements of colours appear
in flight, there is also a revelation of personality.
Study your birds on the ground as you will, but

once you have thus observed them and studied their loveliness, do not be afraid to clap your hands and send them off into the air. They will take no real alarm and will soon forgive you. Watch birds flying.

The tide is going out, and the breakers are shallowing to chiding curls of foam along the edge of the ebb. Gone are the thin-footed, light-winged peoples, the industrious waders, the busy pickup, runabout, and scurry-along folk. South, south with the sun, along bright beaches and across wide bays, south with the sun along the edge of a continent, with heaven knows what ancient mysteries stirring in their tiny minds and what ancient instincts waking in their veins. As I think of the tropical lands to which these birds have flown, I remember walking one night along a tropical beach in Central America. It was late at night, no one was about, the warm, endless, pouring wind shook a sound like rain out of endlessly agitated palms, and a magnificent full moon sailed through the wind over an ocean and a surf that might have been a liquid and greener moonlight. Suddenly, a flock of little birds rose up on the beach from nowhere, wheeled, fell off a little with the wind, and then disappeared completely into the turbulent splendour. I wonder now if you were by any chance Cape Cod sandpipers, little birds!

But now to return to the North Atlantic, the Eastham dunes, and the exchange of species I mentioned earlier in the chapter. As the smaller birds have flown south to their tropics, birds from the arctic north, following the same migrational impulse of the ebbing year, have moved south along the New England coast, and found in the open, deserted Cape a region which is to them a Florida. These birds are the arctic sea ducks, many of them big, heavy, powerful birds, all of them built to stand icy water and icy weather, all of them enclosed in a water-tight pack of feathers which is almost a kind of feather fur. These ducks belong to the subfamily *Fuligulinæ*, the people of the outermost waters, but there are still other arctic visitors, auks, murres, and even guillemots. The region which these birds prefer is the region south of Cape Cod, where the currents of warmer water swirl over the great south shoals. I have for neighbours the three varieties of "scoters," or more familiarly and wrongly "coots," the black-winged coot *Oidemia americana*, the white-winged coot *Oidemia deglandi*, the skunk coot, *Oidemia perspicillata;* I have scaups or blue-billed widgeons, *Marila marila*, dipper ducks, *Charitonetta albeola*, old squaws, *Harelda hyemalis*, eiders, *Somateria dresseri*, king eiders, *Somateria spectabilis*, and others. It is possible that, before the coming of the white man, the number of these winter outer-sea birds in the Cape Cod region exceeded that of the summer birds, but now, alas! the shotgun and the killer had their fun, the winter peoples have been wasted away, and some even exterminated. To-day, the summer birds outnumber their winter kin.

A new danger, moreover, now threatens the birds at sea. An irreducible residue of crude oil, called by refiners "slop," remains in stills after oil distillation, and this is pumped into southbound tankers and emptied far offshore. This wretched pollution floats over large areas, and the birds alight in it and get it on their feathers. They inevitably die. Just how they perish is still something of a question. Some die of cold, for the gluey oil so mats and swabs the thick arctic feathering that creases open through it to the skin above the vitals; others die of hunger as well. Captain George Nickerson of Nauset tells me that he saw an oil-covered eider trying to dive for food off Monomoy, and that the bird was unable to plunge. I am glad to be able to write that the situation is better than it was. Five years ago, the shores of Monomoy peninsula were strewn with hundreds, even thousands, of dead sea fowl, for the tankers pumped out slop as they were passing the shoals—into the very waters, indeed, on which the birds have lived since time began! To-day oil is more the chance fate of the unfortunate individual. But let us hope that all such pollution will presently end.

My beach is empty, but not the ocean beyond. Between the coast guard station and Nauset Light, a "raft" of skunk coots is spending the winter. Patches of white on the forehead and the hind neck of the glossy black head of the male are responsible for this local name. The birds sit in the ocean, just seaward of the surf—the coast guardsmen say there is a shallow close by and shellfish—and the whole raft rises and falls unconcernedly as the swells roll under it. Sometimes a bird will dive through the oncoming ridge of a breaker and emerge casually on the other side;

sometimes a bird will stand up in the water, flap its wings, and settle down again unconcernedly. There are perhaps thirty birds in this flock. In Thoreau's time, these rafts of coots formed a flock which was practically continuous the whole length of the outer Cape, but to-day such rafts, though not at all rare, are but occasional.

Standing at the door of my house, I watch these winter birds pass and repass, flying well offshore. Now a company of a hundred or more old squaws pass, now a tribe of one of the scoter folk; now a pair of eiders come to rest in the ocean directly in front of the Fo'castle.

These birds practically never come ashore during the winter. They eat, sleep, live, and meet together at sea. When you see a sea duck on the beach, you can be sure something is the matter with him, so runs a saying of the Cape which I had from Captain Nickerson. The only way in which I can observe these winter folk is by using a good glass or by catching a specimen who has got into some kind of trouble and taken refuge on the beach. All these creatures are at a great disadvantage when ashore, and have a world of difficulty trying to launch themselves

into the air; they make unwieldy jump after
jump, the auks being practically unable to rise
at all upon their wings. It was thrilling to walk
the beach, and catch sight of a bird sitting solitary on the sands. What might it be? What had
led it ashore? Could I possibly catch it and give
it a careful looking over? The keynote of my
strategy lay in the attempt to prevent the birds
from getting back into the water, so between
them and the surf I would rush—for the birds
would begin to move down the slope to the surf
the instant they saw or heard or felt me—and I
soon learned that a brisk countercharge was
worth all the ruse and the patient stalking in
the world. Then began a furious game of tag, the
alarmed bird skittering all over the beach, being
gradually driven by me toward the dunes, till I
manœuvred him into the angle between the
beach and the sandy wall.

My first prisoners were three unhappy little
auks, *Alle alle*, who had dipped themselves in
oil somewhere on their way down from the arctic
—odd little browny-black and white birds about
the size of a pigeon, who stood up on queer little
auk feet, faced me, and beat little bent wings
with a penguin look to them; indeed, the bird

has much of an Adelie penguin air. On the Cape, these auks are known as "pine knots"—a term said to be derived from the creature's tough compactness—or as "dovekies." They have always been "aukies" to me. At the Fo'castle I gave them a generous corner floored with newspaper and walled in with boards and a chair. I tried to clean off what I could of the oil; I gave them what I could find of sea victuals, but all in vain; they would not eat, and I let them go just as soon as I saw that I could not possibly help them and that Nature had best deal with the problem in her own way.

When they stood up almost perpendicularly and tried to walk about on their little legs set far aft—they are *pygopodes*—it was much as if an acrobat, standing on his head, were trying to patter about, using the length between his elbow and his finger tips as feet. These little birds used both wings and feet when trying to escape me on the beach. They ran and *rowed* the sand with their wings; the verb gives the precise motion. Moreover, what had taken place was beautifully marked upon the *tabula rasa* of the sand—little webbed feet running in a close chain, wing tips nicking the sand once in each stroke.   Coming south from their distant arctic, these little auks do not fly above the ocean as do the more advanced birds; they "skitter" along just over the surface of the waves and keep well out to sea, even well out of sight of land.

One aukie I caught at night. I was on the beach walking north to meet the man coming south from Nauset, and, as I flashed my searchlight to see who the surfman might be, I saw an aukie coming toward me, fluttering along the very edge of surf, all sticky and a-glisten with fuel oil. Strange little fragment of life on the edge of that mysterious immensity! I picked him up; he struggled and then kept still, and I carried him back to the Fo'castle. The bird was small enough to be carried in one hand, and as I held him, his duck feet rested on my palm and his head and neck emerged from the fork between my thumb and index finger. At the Fo'castle he opened his beak, "chattered" with it (there is no word for that motion without sound), transformed his short neck into a surprisingly long one, and looked at me with a kind of "all is well but anything may be expected" expression in his eyes. Every now and then he rather solemnly winked, showing the delicate tan-coloured feathering on his lid. I put him in a corner by himself, and when I went to bed he had given up trying to pick himself free of the oil with his pointed, sparrowy bill, and was standing in his corner of shadow, facing the angle of the walls, for all the world like a small boy who has been naughty at school. The next morning I let him go at his own insistent request.

I found a razor-billed auk, *Alca torda*, cornered him, looked him over while he threatened me with a bill held open and motionless, and then left him to his own devices. I did the same with a Brünnich's murre, and I might have had an eider, too, had I wanted one, for Alvin Newcomb, surf-man No. 1 at Nauset, captured a male one night while on north patrol. The eider, however, is a huge bird, and I was not quite prepared to turn the Fo'castle into a kind of ocean hen yard. So the eider at Nauset, after having most un-concernedly listened to the station radio for a little while, was returned that same evening to the North Atlantic. I had one chance at a rare bird. On the first day of the great northeast storm, as I was wandering about at noontime through the sleet, I found in the mouth of a cut the body of a murre. The bird had been dead but a short time, for it was still limp when I picked it up, and as I held it I could even feel a faint vanishing warmth in its exhausted flesh. This bird was the rarer murre, *Uria troile troile*, he of the sharper beak whom men have almost erased from the list of living things. It had apparently died of being caught and battered about for long hours by the gale. After the storm, I tried to find the creature again, but the tide and the storm had poured through the cut and swept everything before them into a confusion of sand and ruin.

These ocean peoples live on such little fish as they can seize; they pick up shellfish on shallow areas; they eat certain marine growths. Some have a taste for the local mussel, *Mytilus edulis*. Unless the winter is an exceptionally severe one, the birds seem to fare well enough. Many stay late, and May is usually at hand before the long lines of scoters fly north again under the command of their feathered admirals. Such is the history of the migrant seafarers of the Cape. A word remains to be said about the residents and the migrants in the marsh.

II

About the middle of December, I began to see that an amusing game of cross purposes was being played by the sea birds and the land birds of the region west of the dunes. Food becoming scarce upon the uplands, crows, bobwhites, and starlings began to take an interest in the sea and the salt meadows, while gulls took to exploring the moors and to sitting in the top branches of inland pines. One wise old gull once discovered that there was good fare to be had in Mr. Joe Cobb's chicken yard just off the western rim of the great marsh, and every morning this sagacious creature would separate himself from the thousands milling about over the cold tides and flutter down among the hens. There he would forage about, picking up grain like a barnyard fowl till he had dulled the edge of his hunger. I doubt if gulls ever do more. After visiting the chicken yard regularly for several winters, the bird disappeared one spring and was never seen again. He had probably lived out the span of his days.

I pause here to wonder at how little we know of the life span of wild animals. Only cases of exceptionally long life or short life seem to attract the attention of man. I can open any good bird book and find a most careful, a most detailed study of the physical selves and habits of birds, but of their probable length of life, never a word. Such material would be exceedingly difficult to secure, and perhaps the suggestion is folly, but there are times when one wishes that this neglected side of animal existence might have more attention.

During the summer, I never saw starlings on the marsh, but now that winter is here they leave the uplands by the coast guard station, and venture out along the dunes. These flights of exploration are very rare. I have seen the birds flying over the salt meadows, I have seen them light on the ridgepole of a gunning camp, but I have never once encountered them on the outer beach. With crows, it is a different story. The birds will investigate anything promising, and during the summer I found crows on the beach on four or five different occasions, these visits being made, for the most part, early in the morning.

Chancing to look toward the marsh one warm October afternoon, I witnessed a battle between

two gulls and a young crow for the possession of
some marine titbit the crow had picked up on
the flats; it was a picturesque contest, for the
great silvery wings of the gulls beat down and
inclosed the crow till he resembled a junior
demon in some old lithograph of the war in
heaven. Eventually one of the gulls seized on the
coveted morsel, flew off a bit, and gulped it down,
leaving the crow and the other gull to "consider"
like the cow in the old song. Winter and necessity
now make the crow something of a beach
comber. The birds cross over to the beach at
low tide on mild days, forage about warily, and
return to their uplands the instant they no
longer have the beach all to themselves. A flight
of gulls will send them cawing home, their great
sombre wings beating the ocean air. Even on this
immense and lonely beach, they remain the
wariest of creatures, and if I wish to see what
they are up to, I have to use ten times the care
in stalking them that I would have to use in
stalking any casual sea bird. I have to creep
through cuts and valleys in the dunes and worm
my way over cold sand that drinks the warmth
and life out of the flesh. I usually find them picking at a fish flung out of the breakers perhaps a

day or two before—picking industriously and solemnly.

Once in a while, a covey of shore larks will cross the dunes and alight on the beach in the lee and the afternoon shadow of the sand bank. They fly very low, the whole group rising and falling with the rise and fall of the hills and hollows, a habit that gives their flights a picturesque and amusing roller-coaster quality. Once having settled down on the outer side of the dunes, the birds keep well up on the beach and never seem to venture close to ocean.

This same shore lark, *Otocoris alpestris*, is perhaps the bird I encounter most frequently during the winter months. This season they are here by the thousand; indeed, they are so thick that I scarce can walk behind the dunes without putting up a flock of these alert, brownish, fugitive creatures. Their kingdom lies to the west of the dunes, in the salt-hay fields and intermingled marsh areas which extend between the dunes and the creek running more or less parallel to the sand bar. Coming from Greenland and Labrador, these birds reach the Eastham meadows in October and November, and all winter long they forage and run about in the dead bristles of the hay. Their only note here is a rather sad little "*tseep, tseep,*" which they utter as they skim the grass in alarm, but it is said that they have an interesting song during their breeding season in springtime Labrador.

It is early on a pleasant winter afternoon, and I am returning to the Fo'castle through the meadows, my staff in my hand and a load of groceries in a knapsack on my back. The preceding day brought snow flurries to us out of the northwest, and there are patches of snow on the hay fields and the marshes, and, on the dunes, nests of snow held up off the ground by wiry spears of beach grass bent over and tangled into a cup. Such little pictures as this last are often to be seen on the winter dunes; I pause to enjoy them, for they have the quality and delicacy of Japanese painting. There is a blueness in the air, a blue coldness on the moors, and across the sky to the south, a pale streamer of cloud smoking from its upper edge. Every now and then, I see ahead of me a round, blackish spot in the thin snow; these are the cast-off shells of horseshoe crabs, from whose thin tegument the snow has melted. A flock of nervous shore larks, hidden under an old mowing machine, emerge running,

take to their wings, and, flying south a fifty
yards, suddenly drop and disappear into the
grass. Hesitating on the half-alert, a little flock
of bobwhites, occasional invaders of this stubble,
watch me pass, and then continue feeding. To
the west, from the marsh, I hear the various
cries of gulls, the mewing note, the call, and that
queer sound which is almost a guttural bark.
Afternoon shadows are gathering in the cuts of
the dunes, blue shadows and cold, and there is a
fine sea tang in the air.

It is low tide, and the herring gulls, *Larus
argentatus*, are feeding on the flats and gravel
banks. As I watch them through a glass, they
seem as untroubled as fowls on an inland farm.
Their talkative groups and gatherings have
a domestic look. The gull population of the
Cape is really one people, for, though separate
gull congregations live in various bays and
marshes, the mass of the birds seem to hear of
any new food supply and flock as one
to the feast. So accustomed to man have
they grown, and so fearless, that they will
follow in his very footsteps for a chance to
scavenge food; I have seen the great birds walking round clammers who threw broken clams to

them as they might throw scraps of meat to kittens. In hungry seasons the clammer may hear a flapping just behind and discover that a gull has just made off with a clam from his pail. They follow the eelers, too, and on the ice of the Eastham salt pond you may chance to see a pair of gulls disputing an eel which the eelers have thrown away; one will have it by the tail, the other by the head, and both tug with insistence and increasing bad temper. The victory in this primitive battle goes either to the strongest gull or to the fastest swallower.

An unhurried observation of the marsh, especially a study of its lesser creeks and concealed pools, reveals hundreds of ducks. To identify and classify these birds is a next to impossible task, for they are very suspicious and have chosen their winter quarters with a sound instinct for defensive strategy. The great majority of these birds are undoubtedly black duck, *Anas rubripes*, the most wary and suspicious of all wintering birds. All day long, back and forth over the dunes between the marsh and the ocean, these ducks are ever flying; by twos and threes and little flocks they go, and those who go out to sea fly so far out that the eye loses them in the vastness of ocean. I like to walk in the marsh early in the evening, keeping out as far as I can toward the creeks. The ducks hear me and begin a questioning quacking. I hear them talk and take alarm; other ducks, far off, take up the *alerte;* sometimes wings whistle by in the darkness. The sound of a pair of "whistler" ducks on the wing is a lovely, mysterious sound at such a time. It is a sound made with wings, a clear, sibilant note which increases as the birds draw near, and dies away in the distance like a faint and whistling sigh.

One March evening, just as sundown was fading into night, the whole sky chanced to be overspread with cloud, all save a golden channel in the west between the cloud floor and the earth. It was very still, very peaceful on my solitary dune. The whole earth was dark, dark as a shallow cup lifted to a solemnity of silence and cloud. I heard a familiar sound. Turning toward the marsh, I saw a flock of geese flying over the meadows along the rift of dying, golden light, their great wings beating with a slow and solemn beauty, their musical, bell-like cry filling the lonely levels and the dark. Is there a nobler wild clamour in all the world? I listened to the sound till it died away and the birds had disappeared into darkness, and then heard a quiet sea chiding a little at the turn of tide. Presently, I began to feel a little cold, and returned to the Fo'castle, and threw some fresh wood on the fire.

Chapter VI

LANTERNS ON THE BEACH

I

It is now the middle of March, cold winds stream between earth and the serene assurance of the sun, winter retreats, and for a little season the whole vast world here seems as empty as a shell. Winter is no mere negation, no mere absence of summer; it is another and a positive presence, and between its ebbing and the slow, cautious inflow of our northern spring there is a phase of earth emptiness, half real, perhaps, and half subjective. A day of rain, another bright week, and all earth will be filled with the tremor and the thrust of the year's new energies.

There has just been a great wreck, the fifth this winter and the worst. On Monday morning last, shortly after five o'clock, the big three-masted schooner *Montclair* stranded at Orleans and went to pieces in an hour, drowning five of her crew.

It had blown hard all Sunday night, building up enormous seas. Monday's dawn, however, was not stormy, only wintry and grey. The *Montclair*, on her way from Halifax to New York, had had a hard passage, and sunrise found her off Orleans with her rigging iced up and her crew dog-weary. Helpless and unmanageable, she swung inshore and presently struck far out and began to break up. Lifted, rocked, and pounded by the morning's mountainous seas, her masts were seen to quiver at each crash, and presently her foremast and her mainmast worked free, and, scissoring grotesquely back and forth across each other, split the forward two thirds of the vessel lengthwise—"levered the ship open," as Russell Taylor of Nauset said. The vessel burst, the two forward masses of the ship drifted inshore and apart, a cargo of new laths poured into the seas from the broken belly of the hold. Seven men clung to the rocking, drifting mass that was once the stern.

It was a singular fragment, for the vessel had broken as neatly crosswise as it had lengthwise, and the seas were washing in below deck as into an open barrel. Dragging over the shoal ground, the mass rocked on its keel, now rolling the men sickeningly high, now tumbling them down into the trampling rush of the seas. The fall of the two forward masts had snapped off the mizzen some twenty-five feet above the deck, and from the stump cracked-out slivers swung free with the rolling. Bruised, wet through, and chilled to the bone, the unfortunate men dared not lash themselves down, for they had to be free to climb the tilted deck when the ship careened.

Five clung to the skylight of the after deck-house, two to the stern-rail balustrade. Laths filled the sea, poured over the men, and formed a jagged and fantastic wall along the beach.

One great sea drowned all the five. Men on the beach saw it coming and shouted, the men on the deckhouse shouted and were heard, and then the wave broke, hiding the tragic fragment in a sluice of foam and wreckage. When this had poured away, the men on the afterhouse were gone. A head was visible for a minute, and then another drifting southward, and then there was nothing but sea.

Two men still clung to the balustrade, one a seventeen-year-old boy, the other a stocky, husky-built sailor. The wave tore the boy from the balustrade, but the stocky man reached out, caught him, and held on. The tide rising, the stern began to approach the beach. A detail of men hurriedly sent over from Nauset Station now appeared on the beach and managed to reach and rescue the survivors. The *Montclair* had chanced to strand near a station classed as "inactive"—coast guard stations are discontinued if there is not enough work to justify their maintenance—and the two or three men who garrisoned the station could do little but summon instant aid. Men came from Nauset, circling the Eastham lagoon and Orleans cove in local automobiles, but the whole primitive tragedy was over in a moment of time.

As the vessel was breaking up, men came to the beach and helped themselves to the laths and what wreckage they fancied. Later on, there was a kind of an auction of the salvaged material. The other day I saw half-a-dozen bundles of the *Montclair's* laths piled up near a barn.

A week after the wreck, a man walking the Orleans shore came to a lonely place, and there he saw ahead of him a hand thrust up out of the great sands. Beneath he found the buried body of one of the *Montclair's* crew.

I can see the broken mast of the schooner from the deck of the Fo'castle. Sunday last, I walked over to the ship. The space under the after deckhouse from which the men were swept—officers, quarters, I imagine—is an indescribable flung mass of laths, torn wood, wrecked panelling, sopped blankets, and sailor's clothing. I remember the poor, stringy, cheap ties. In the midst of the débris a stain of soppy pink paper caught my eye: it was a booklet, "If You Were Born in February." I have often seen the set of twelve on newsstands. The scarlet cover of this copy had seeped into the musty pages. "Those who are born in this month," I read, "have a particular affection for home"; and again, "They will go through fire and water for their loved ones."

Who brought this thing aboard? one wonders. Whose curious hands first opened it in the lamplight of this tragic and disordered space? The seventeen-year-old boy is dead of the shock and exposure; the stocky, husky-built man, the only survivor, is going on with the sea. "He says it's all he knows," said a coast guardsman.

The wreck lies on the edge of the surf and trembles when the incoming seas strike its counter and burst there with a great upflinging of heavy spray.

II

To understand this great outer beach, to appreciate its atmosphere, its "feel," one must have a sense of it as the scene of wreck and elemental drama. Tales and legends of the great disasters fill no inconsiderable niche in the Cape mind. Older folk will tell you of the *Jason*, of how she struck near Pamet in a gale of winter rain, and of how the breakers flung the solitary survivor on the midnight beach; others will tell of the tragic *Castagna* and the frozen men who were taken off while the snow flurries obscured the February sun. Go about in the cottages, and you may sit in a chair taken from one great wreck and at a table taken from another; the cat purring at your feet may be himself a rescued mariner. When the coast guards returned to the *Castagna* on the quiet morning after the wreck, they found a grey cat calmly waiting for them in the dead captain's cabin, and a chilled canary hunched up upon his perch. The bird died of the bitter cold while being taken ashore in a life-boat, "just fell off," but the cat left a dynasty to carry on his name.

Cape Codders have often been humorously reproached for their attitude toward wrecks. On this coast, as on every other in the old isolated days, a wreck was treasure trove, a free gift of the sea; even to-day, the usable parts of a wreck are liable to melt away in a curious manner. There is no real looting; in fact, public opinion on the Cape is decidedly against such a practice, for it offends the local sense of decency. The gathering of the *Montclair's* laths during the wreck really upset many people. They did not like it here. When men are lost on the beach, the whole Cape takes it very much to heart, talks about it, mulls over it; when men are saved, there is no place where they are treated with greater hospitality and kindness. Cape folks have never been wreckers in the European sense of that dark word. Their first thought has always been of the shipwrecked men.

Forty years ago, a winter nor'easter flung the schooner *J. H. Eells* on the outer bar of Eastham. Water-logged, leaking, and weighted down with a cargo of railroad iron, the ship remained on the outer bar, snow flurries hiding her now and then through the furious winter day. So swift and powerful were the alongshore currents that a surfboat could not approach the ship, and so far offshore had she stranded that the life-saving gun would not carry. All Eastham was on the beach, the women as well as the boys and men, and all day long villagers and surfmen fought to reach the vessel. They were powerless, however, and when darkness and continuing snow closed the winter day, they had to watch the *Eells* fading away in the squalls, her dying men still clinging to the shrouds.

To give these men heart, to let them know themselves remembered, the villagers that night built great fires of driftwood on the beach. Men and women shook the thin snow and sand from ancient wreckage and tossed it on a wind-crazed heap of flame. All night long they fed these pyres. With the slow return of day, it was seen that two of the men had already died and fallen overboard. At ten o'clock that morning, the storm having somewhat abated, the survivors were pluckily taken off by a lone tug which approached the wreck from seaward. Every once in a while, the rusty, shell-fouled iron uncovers, and above it, the yellow-green waters of the outer bar turn blue-black in a strike of summer sun.

Eighteenth Century pirates, stately British

merchantmen of the mid-Victorian years, whaling brigs, Salem East India traders, Gloucester fishermen, and a whole host of forgotten Nineteenth Century schooners—all these have strewn this beach with broken spars and dead. Why this history of wreck and storm? Because the outer Cape stands a full thirty miles out in the North Atlantic, and because its shelterless eastern beaches flank the New Englander's ocean lanes for fifty miles. When a real nor'easter blows, howling landward through the winter night over a thousand miles of grey, tormented seas, all shipping off the Cape must pass the Cape or strand. In the darkness and scream of the storm, in the beat of the endless, icy, crystalline snow, rigging freezes, sails freeze and tear—of a sudden the long booming undertone of the surf sounds under the lee bow—a moment's drift, the feel of surf twisting the keel of the vessel, then a jarring, thundering crash and the upward drive of the bar.

Stranded vessels soon begin to break up. Wrecks drag and pound on the shoals, the waves thunder in-board, decks splinter and crack like wooden glass, timbers part, and iron rods bend over like candles in a heat.

Ships may strand here in dull weather and
fog. The coast guards then work at full speed to
get them off before a surf rises; a coast guard
cutter comes to aid.

A few mornings ago, when I walked the beach
to Nauset Station, I followed close along the dune
wall to see the wreckage uncovered since the
storm. North of the Fo'castle, along a broken
mile, the new seaward cliff of the dunes stands
at least twenty feet west of the former rim, and
all the old wreckage once buried up in the region
washed away is now lying on the beach or tumbling out of the wall. Being young, the twelve-
foot cliff is still sheer, and the wreckage lies
solidly packed in its side like fruits in a sliced pud-
ding. In one place, some ten feet of a schooner's
mast is jutting from the wall like a cannon from
a fortress; in another, the sand is crumbling
away from the fragments of a ship's boat, in
another appears the speckled and musty yellow
corner of a door. Root tendrils of beach grass,
whitish and fine-spun as open nerves, have
grown in the crumbled and sand-eroded crevices.

Some of this wreckage is centuries old. High
course tides carry débris up the beach, sand and
the dunes move down to claim it; presently

beach grass is growing tall in sand wedged between a ship's splintered ribs and its buried keel. A few laths from the *Montclair* are whitening on the beach.

Two miles down the beach, its tiny flag streaming seaward in the endless wind, stands Nauset Station, chimneys, weathered roof, and cupola watchtower just visible above the dunes.

III

From Monomoy Point to Race Point in Provincetown—full fifty miles—twelve coast guard stations watch the beach and the shipping night and day. There are no breaks save natural ones in this keep of the frontier.

Between the stations, at some midway and convenient point, stand huts called halfway houses, and stations, huts, and lighthouses are linked together by a special telephone system owned and maintained by the coast guard services.

Every night in the year, when darkness has fallen on the Cape and the sombre thunder of ocean is heard in the pitch pines and the moors, lights are to be seen moving along these fifty miles of sand, some going north, some south, twinkles and points of light solitary and mysterious. These lights gleam from the lanterns and electric torches of the coast guardsmen of the Cape walking the night patrols. When the nights are full of wind and rain, loneliness and the thunder of the sea, these lights along the surf have a quality of romance and beauty that is Elizabethan, that is beyond all stain of present time.

Sometimes a red flare burns on the edge of ocean, a red fireworks flare which means wreck or danger of wreck. "You are standing in too near to the outer bar," says the red light to the freighter lost in a night's downpour of March rain. "Keep off! Keep off! Keep off!" The signal burns and sputters, the smoke is blown away almost ere it is born; the glassy bellies of the advancing breakers turn to volutes of rosy black, the seething foam to a strange vermilion-pink. In the night and rain beyond the hole of light an answering bellow sounds, ship lights dim as the vessel changes her course, the red flare dies to a sizzling, empty cartridge, the great dark of the beach returns to the solitary dunes. The next day it is all entered quietly in the station log: "Two thirty-six A. M. saw freighter standing in toward outer bar, burnt Coston signals, freighter whistled and changed her course."

Every night they go; every night of the year the eastern beaches see the comings and goings of the wardens of Cape Cod. Winter and summer they pass and repass, now through the midnight sleet and fury of a great northeaster, now through August quiet and the reddish-golden radiance of an old moon rising after midnight from the sea, now through a world of rain shaken with heavy thunder and stabbed through and through with lightning. And always, always alone. Whenever I rise at earliest dawn, I find the beach traced and retraced with footprints that vanish in the distances, each step a chain forged anew each night in the courageous service of mankind.

Night patrols go between the stations and their halfway houses. Under certain circumstances and at special times of the year, the last patrol in the morning may end at a key post placed on some commanding height above the beach. While on patrol, the men carry a stock of red flare cartridges—the Coston lights—a handle to burn them in, and a watchman's clock which they must wind with a special key kept at the halfway house. In summer, the beaches are covered twice every night, in winter three times, the first patrol leaving the station soon after dark, the second at midnight, the third an hour or so before the dawn. The average patrol covers something like seven miles. Only one man from each station is on the beach at any given time, so north and south patrols alternate through the night.

Day patrols are maintained only during stormy or foggy weather. The men then have to walk the beach night and day with not much chance for proper rest, mile after mile of a furious winter day on the heels of a long and almost sleepless night. The usual day watch is kept from the towers of the stations.

A surfman who has discovered a wreck or found some sort of trouble on the beach first burns the Coston light I have already mentioned. This warns his station that there is something the matter, and at the same time tells men aboard a wreck that they have been seen and that help is coming. If the wreck lies near the station, the guard returns with his news; if it lies near the halfway house, he telephones. At the station, the man on station watch gives the alarm, everybody tumbles up, and in the quickest possible time the crew and their apparatus are on the beach hurrying through the darkness to the wreck. Each station has now a small tractor to draw its apparatus down the beach.

The crew of a stranded ship may be taken off either in the lifeboat or the breeches buoy. Everything depends on the conditions of the hour.

The life-saving cannon and its auxiliary apparatus, its powder, lines, hawsers, and pulleys, are kept in a stout two-wheeled wagon called "the beach cart." The "shot," or projectile, fired from this gun resembles a heavy brass window weight with one end pulled out into a stout two-foot rod ending in a loop.

When a wreck lies offshore in the surf, the end of a very light line called the "shot line" is attached to the eyelet in the brass projectile, and the gun aimed at the wreck with particular care. One must place the shot where the men in the rigging can reach it, and yet avoid striking them. If all goes well, the shot whizzes into the very teeth of the gale and falls aboard, leaving the shot line entangled. Should the wrecked men succeed in reaching and hauling in this first cord, a heavier line is sent on, and when the mariners haul in this second line, "the whip," they haul out to their vessel the lifebuoy and its hawser. Pulleys and cables are so rigged as to permit the buoy to be hauled in and out to the wreck by the coast guard crew.

After everybody has been taken off, an ingenious contrivance is hauled out to the wreck which cuts the hawser free. The crew then gather up the apparatus, station a guard, and return.

The crew return, the little group of men in black oilers and the men they have saved trudge off, tunnelling into the wind, the surfboat on its wagon-cradle leading the way, the hum-rhythm of the tractor dissolving in the gale. Ridges and piles of broken, twisted wreckage rim the breakers' edges, new wreckage is on its way ashore, strewings of old weathered planking, a hatchway, sops of sailors' clothing. A maze of footprints traces the desolate beach; the air is full of wind-flung froth and breaker spray; the gale screams unceasing. Just offshore, in the mile of surf, the wreck lies flat—utterly forlorn, and helpless as a toy ship neglected by a giant's child. The guard left behind walks to and fro, rubs his mittened hands, and watches the breakers cover the wreck under mountains of surf, overflow, and sluice off in spouting masses and cascades . . . breaking up . . . Fishing schooner, rigging frozen up, one of the men with both his hands frozen . . . yes, got 'em all.

IV

I call at Nauset Station several times a week, usually late in the afternoon. Packages and mail are delivered near by, and every once in a while I call there for a message sent on to me from Eastham.

The station stands on the mainland of the Cape just where the dunes begin; it is a white wooden building built snug and low like a Cape Cod cottage; indeed, it rather resembles a Cape cottage in its design. On the ground floor is the boat room, a kitchen-dining room, a living room, and the captain's quarters; on the floor above are two dormitory spaces. From the west dormitory, a ship's ladder leads through a trapdoor to the tower.

My neighbours of Nauset live there much as men might on a small vessel. They have drills and duties, their definite enlistments—the first enlistment is for three years—their pay days, their service discipline, their uniforms, and days

of leave. Breakfast at seven, drills in the morning
—surfboat drill to-day, resuscitation drill or
blinker and flag drill to-morrow—dinner at
eleven, tower watch in turn through all the day,
sleep and recreation in the late afternoon, supper
at four-thirty, then sundown, night, and the long
miles of loneliness and ocean. In winter the guards
wear a uniform of dark navy blue and a blue
flannel shirt; in summer they shift into sailor
whites, broad collar, white hat, and all. Officially,
the men are known as "surfmen" and are ranked
by number according to their standing and length
of service.

A fine group, these wardens of the Cape. Into
the worst storm they go—without a question,
with never a hesitation—a storm in which life
would seem impossible. The door clangs behind
them, the sleet screams at the windows, the very
earth of the old Cape shakes to the thunder of
the seas, but they are already on the moors,
fighting on into the gale; fighting on, crawling on,
for seven dreadful miles. Yet the men make
nothing of it and scarcely ever talk about it—
they simply take their black oilskins and rubber
boots from a locker, get into them by lantern
light, and go.

I owe the Nauset crew a very genuine debt. Without their friendly interest and aid, without their hospitality and continuing good-will, my experiment might well have been both over-solitary and difficult. Those long winter nights in the lamplit domesticity of my house, the rising wail of the wind on the dunes, the flash of the surfman's light in the whirls of snow, the moment's reunion with mankind, the pause on the beach, the moment's talk by the fire—all that is written deep. The winter long, in foul weather, I kept a night lamp burning in a window and a pot of coffee a-simmer on the hearth. Sometimes I heard steps on the little deck of the Fo'castle, sometimes no one came, and the light guttered out unvisited in the dawn.

The majority of my neighbours are of Cape Cod stock. Born of Cape blood and reared in the Cape atmosphere, even men who have never been to sea have an instinctive turn for the sea and the ways of ships. But these wardens of the Cape are not sailors ashore; they are "surfmen." The name is a wise one—men of the great beach, inheritors of a long, local tradition concerning surf and all its ways. These men have heard the roar of the great beach sounding about their cradles. As I have already written, the sight of the surf in a great gale on the Cape is a spectacle of mingled exaltation, magnificence, and terror, while to venture it in a boat would strike any landsman as a lunatic performance. On such occasions, the sound, traditional surf knowledge of Cape men comes into play. Captains of coast guard crews here choose their launching ground, choose their moment, choose their wave. All together now, go!—and out she runs, the captain standing astern, facing the breakers and steering, the men pulling for their lives.

v

Five o'clock in the afternoon, and I have arrived at Nauset Station after a walk up the beach in a cold head-wind. I slip my pack from my back and stand my beach staff in a corner of the little entry way outside the kitchen door. The great storm tore down so much of the bank that the water in the kitchen well now has an odd taste to it, and the men have had to bring drinking water from the village; a ship's cask and a spring-water bottle stand on the entry floor. In the pink-buff walls are various locker doors. The four-thirty supper is drawing to a close, but my neighbours are still at table, for I can hear voices and discussion at the board. I know each familiar tone. Having an ancient prejudice against disturbing friends at meals, I wait a little while . . . the minutes pass . . . I knock at the kitchen door.

Come in! I find my friends still at their long table at the kitchen's farther end. Supper is just about over. Somebody went fishing yesterday, and on the table a great tureen, once full of good fish chowder, stands at dead low tide. . . . Sit down and have a cup of coffee with us. . . . Thanks, I'd love to. . . . Follows a shoving about of chairs to make room, and presently I am seated at the board, talking beach gossip, eating coast guard doughnuts, and sipping brown-black coffee from a giant white coffee cup of the armour-plate variety. The good hot "mug-up" of coffee, thus hospitably poured, is pleasant after my long, cold walk. My table mates are all young men, some of them scarce more than strapping boys on the threshold of the twenties. Here are the names of my hosts: Captain George B. Nickerson, Commanding Officer; Alvin Newcomb, Surfman No. 1; Russell Taylor, No. 2; Zenas Adams, No. 3; William Eldredge, No. 4; Andrew

Wetherbee, No. 5; Albert Robbins, No. 6; Everett Gross, No. 7; Malcolm Robbins, No. 8; Effin Chalke, No. 9. Other old friends have finished their enlistments or been transferred—Wilbur Chase, John Blood, Kenneth Young, and Yngve Rongner, who gave me my swordfish sword.

The captains of the various stations are well-known men and rank high in the community. When I first came to Eastham, Nauset was under the command of my kind friend Captain Abbott H. Walker, an expert among surfmen and boatmen, and one of the best liked and most respected men on all Cape Cod. Two years ago, after having been in command of Nauset for twenty-six stirring years, he retired to his pleasant house on Orleans Bay. The station was fortunate in having as his successor a distinguished younger officer, Captain George B. Nickerson of Chatham. Nauset is a busy station, and Captain Nickerson has already added new laurels to its splendid history.

The table talk is good, the speech racy and vigorous. Sipping coffee, I hear of a battle at sea fought that very morning between some large unknown fish and unseen enemies—"right off the station"—the fish leaping clear, a great wound or spot visible in its side. . . . Here, have another cup. . . .

"No, going out in a gale isn't as bad as facing 'the sand.' Rather face a nor'easter any time."

Every once in a while, usually in autumn, a dry, gale will descend upon the beach and stir up a sandstorm worthy of the Sahara. I chanced to see such a storm three years ago. The simoon began, I remember, with a sunset of fiery rose deepening to smoky carmine, the sky being empty save for a few thin, sailing wisps. With the smouldering out of this strange sky and the arrival of starlight, a north wind which had blown vigorously all day was taken over by a devil. It shifted its quarter, began to blow directly down the beach, and increased enormously in force. Within half an hour, the whole world of beach and dune was one screaming, smoky, inhuman arabia of flying sand. Sucking up the sand from strewn miles of driftage, tearing at the roots of everything movable, the wind torrent rushed along the beach as down a channel. Presently pebbles, sticks, barrel staves, sides of old fruit crates, hoops, tufts of whipped-out beach grass, clots of breaker spume, and a world of nameless dark lumps joined the general rush through the demoniac and smothering gloom. I myself sailed before the storm, my head turtled down into the very shoulders of a canvas coat, my eyes blinking and painful from the stabs of sand, my nostrils hot and dry with the breathing of it, my mouth much occupied in spitting out grits. And I wondered who was on north patrol that night—walking into it, his head turned sideways and down, and a board held up before his face.

Once upon a time, so runs a service story, a surfman was walking the beach on one of these nights of sand when he heard behind him a strange and uncanny moan. Startled, he turned round, squinted for a second into the gale, and saw coming toward him a great, dark, bounding thing which moaned as it ran. The surfman ran. The thing followed, gaining every instant and sounding its ghostly cry. Out of breath at last, the fugitive fell flat, caught hold of the sand, and gasped out this valedictory, "If ye want me, come and git me." A moment later, an enormous empty cask rolled over the prostrate figure and disappeared down the beach toward Monomoy. The bung halfway up its side was open, and every time the hole had rolled up into the wind, the whistling moan had terrified the night.

Who goes first south to-night? Malcolm Robbins, he goes first south, and Long, he goes at two-thirty.

Time to tidy up. Each man carries his plate and cutlery to the sink, the cook of the day puts on coal, there is talk, the vigorous clank of the kitchen pump, the sound of a dish pan filling, a smell of pipe tobacco. The surfman who has been on watch in the station tower during the meal comes in and eats alone at the cleared-off and deserted board. Clatter of dish and spoon . . . voices. Baseball prospects? Radio news? Station happenings? Somebody opens a window on the last of the chill spring afternoon, and suddenly, in an unexpected instant of quiet, I hear the thundering overspill and ebbing roar of a single giant sea.

Chapter *VII*

AN INLAND STROLL IN SPRING

I

I woke last night just after two o'clock and found my larger room brimming with April moonlight and so still that I could hear the ticking of my watch. Unable and half unwilling to sleep again, I dressed and went out upon the dunes. When something wakes me thus at night, I often dress and go quietly forth on an exploring expedition. It was mildly cold in my ocean world, a light westerly breeze was flowing in fitful eddies close along the earth, the moon was full and high in a cloudless heaven, the surf was but a wash along the ebb. Staff in hand, I crossed the beach to the good footing along the water's edge, and walked south at a slow pace toward big dune.

As I approached the shadow of the dune, I heard from behind it, and ever so faint and high and far away, a sound in the night. The sound began to approach and to increase in its wild music, and after what seemed a long minute, I heard it again from somewhere overhead and a little out to sea. I stared into the sky but could see nothing; the sound that I had heard died away. Again from behind the dune and to the west of south I heard the lovely, broken, chorusing, bell-like sound—the sound of a great flight of geese going north on a quiet night under the moon.

I climbed big dune then, the peak of these sand mountains; the moon shadow was dark upon its eastern slope, but the crest was lifted to the light and commanded both marsh and sea. The channels were still as moonlit forest lakes, the sea was a great deep surfaced with a thin moon splendour of golden green. I lingered there till the moon began to pale, listening to the wild music of the great birds, for a river of life was flowing that night across the sky. Over the elbow of the Cape came the flights, crossing Eastham marsh and the dunes on their way to the immensity of space above the waters. There were little flights and great flights, there were times when the sky seemed empty, there were times when it was filled with an immense clamour which died away slowly over ocean. Not unfrequently I heard the sound of wings, and once in a while I could see the birds—they were flying fast—but scarce had I marked them ere they dwindled into a dot of moonlit sky.

An April morning follows, spring walks upon the dunes, but ocean lingers on the edge of winter. Day after day the April sun pours an increasing splendour on the ocean plain, a hard, bright splendour of light, but the Atlantic mirror drinks no warmth. A chance cloud upon the sun, a shadow, and the sea of an instant returns to February. No shadow of cloud may do the same upon the dunes. Under this April light the mound and landward slopes of the great wall have put on a strange and lovely colour which lies upon them with the delicacy of a reflection in a pool. This colour is a tint of palest olive, even such a ghost of it as one may see in spring on the hill-sides of Provence, and it is born of the mingling of pale sand, blanched grass, and new grass spears of a certain eager green.

The birds of outer ocean, the "coots" or scoters, the old squaws, dipper ducks, eiders and widgeons, the auks and their kin, have practically all of them forsaken the Cape and returned to their breeding grounds in the North. After the fifteenth of April these sea peoples are rarely encountered on the Cape. The lakes of Manitoba are theirs, the glacial hillocks of Greenland and the matted grasses of the tundra. The spring migrations here do not fill the air and the hours with birds as do the autumnal visitations. Urged on by their own imperious instinct and Nature's general will, the creatures have a hurried air, and night flights are more frequent with them than on the southward journeyings.

The first shore birds to pause here on their way back to the Northern country were "ringnecks" —the semipalmated plover, *Charadrius semipalmatus*—and even as the last shore birds I saw were strays, so were these first solitaries and adventurers. On April 2d, I saw a single ringneck running ahead of me along the upper beach; on the 5th I met with another stray; on the 8th I put up a flock of twelve. I have since encountered flocks on several occasions, and sent them wheeling off above the breakers, uttering their melodious and plaintive cry. The note is much like that of the piping plover, *Charadrius melodus*, but without the piping plover's flutelike purity of tone.

Since April 5th a small company of gannets, *Moris bassana*, have been fishing just off the Fo'castle. Gannets have long been favourites of mine. The word "white," applied to the plumage of birds, covers a multitude of minor tintings; some birds are yellowish white, some greyish white, some ivory white, some white with an undertone of rose. To my eye, the gannet wears as pure and as positive a white as one may find in nature, and, moreover, the black tips of his wings are a black past excelling. The bird is large— ornithologists grant him a length between thirty- three and forty inches—and he has a way of using his wings as if they were hinged fins. When sea and sky are a pleasant midday blue, it is a charm- ing bit of life and decorative colour to see these creatures diving. They make a famous plunge. The birds off the Fo'castle, as far as I can judge, hover between forty and fifty feet above the sea and are fishing the shallows on a bar. On catch- ing sight of fish, they fall on the prey like arrows from a cloud. The impact of each body strikes a tiny fountain from the sea. When fish are plenti- ful on the bar, these living plummets fall, climb, and fall again till the whole fishing ground is sown with darts of spray. Like the ringnecks, these gannets are on their way North to the breeding grounds.

Early in March, my friend Kenneth Young of Orleans brought me down a load of groceries in his Ford, and as we stood talking on the porch of the Fo'castle I called his attention to the ducks who were stirring about that morning in the channels and making an unusual noise. "Surely," said I, "they are not beginning to mate so early in the year." "Well, not exactly," said my friend, "but they're 'choosing partners.'" Somehow or other, much of the etiquette, of the "tone" of courtship among gregarious birds has been caught in this phrase born of the older dance; it has a flavour of the bowings and noddings, the showing offs, the coy approaches, the coy escapes, the expected pursuits, the endless conversational whistlings, mewings, squawkings, and quackings which cover the primitive tensity under the politeness.

Under this April blue, the great marshes are emptier of life than I have ever known them; no longer do westerly winds carry to my ears a sound of spring and wooing. The marsh ducks have sought their ponds and wilderness lakes, the larks have climbed the sky to Labrador, even the herring gulls are scattering. Though the breeding season of the latter bird does not begin till the first or second week in May, the marriageable are already wandering east to Maine. Hundreds of isles and islets on the Maine coast are as wild to-day as they were when Champlain visited the archipelago, and the herring gull breeds there by the twice ten thousands.

The sand has entirely resumed its looseness, its fluidity, but its colour still tells of winter in a faintest hint of grey. The golden warmth is there and is emerging; the climbing sun will soon exorcise this ghost of cold. Through the winter flows and spreadings of the sand, the new spears of dune grass rise, the leaves rolled into a green poignard with a tip of rhubarb bed and a terminal spike as piercing as a thorn. Other leaves, other spikes grow from the withered fists of the old plant, and what are left of last year's leaves now crack from brittleness and drop away. Even the oozy vegetation of the flats is sharing in the spring. At dead low tide the streaming eel grass of the channel beds, *Zostera marina*, reveals new patches of wet, bright yellow-green; these stains dominate the spring colours of my world and are very beautiful to see when the April sun is shining.

Mammalian life was the first to emerge from the sterility of winter—I found skunk tracks on the dunes after the certain warm nights in March —and after the mammals came returning birds. Insect life has scarce stirred, though a few stray unknown flies have made their way into the house. In that kingdom life must begin again from the beginning.

April and the sun advancing, the disk rising each day to the north of where it leaped from yesterday's ocean and setting north of yesterday's setting, the solar disk burning, burning, consuming winter in fire.

II

I devoted the entire day yesterday to an adventure I have long had in mind, a walk across the Cape from outer ocean to Cape Cod Bay. As the crow flies, the distance from the Fo'castle to the west shore is about four and a half miles; afoot and by the road, it is nearer seven and a half, for one must follow roads lying north of the great lagoon. The day was pleasant; cool, easterly winds blew across the moors, and it was warm enough when I found both shelter and the sun.

I walked to Nauset Station close along the landward edge of the dunes, out of sight and sound of the sea. All up and down these western gradients of grass and sand the plant life of the region is pushing through the surface drifts and sandy overflowings which crept eastward during winter; green leaves of the beach pea are thrusting up; sand crumbs still lodged in their unfolded crevices; the dune goldenrod is shouldering the bright particles aside. Against the new olive colouring of the dunes, the compact thickets of beach plum are as charred-looking as ever, but when I stroll over to a thicket I find its buds tipped with a tiny show of green.

Arriving at Nauset, I found my coast guard neighbours airing their bedding and cleaning house. Andrew Wetherbee hailed me from the tower; we shouted pleasantries and passed the time of day. Then down Nauset road I went, turning my back on ocean and a rising tide.

The first mile of the road from Nauset to Eastham village winds through a singular country. It is a belt of wild, rolling, and treeless sand moorland which follows along the rim of the earth cliff for two thirds of its length and runs inland for something like a mile. Nauset Station, with its tiny floor of man-made greenery, lies at the frontier between my dune world and this sea-girt waste. Coast guard paths and the low, serried poles of the coast guard telephone are the only clues to the neighbourhood of man.

Desolate and half desert as it is, this borderland of the Cape has an extraordinary beauty, and for me the double attraction of mystery and wide horizons. Just to the north of the station, the grass turns starveling and thin, and the floor of the border waste becomes a thick carpet of poverty grass, *Hudsonia tomentosa*, variegated with channels and starry openings of whitish sand. All winter long this plant has been a kind of a rag grey; it has had a clothlike look and feel, but now it wears one of the rarest and loveliest greens in nature. I shall have to use the term "sage green" in telling of it, but the colour is not so simply ticketed; it is sage green, yes, but of an unequalled richness and sable depth. All along the waste, the increasing light is transmuting the grey sand of winter to a mellowness of grey-white touched with silver; the moor blanches, the plant puts on the dark. To my mind this wild region is at its best in twilight, for its dun floor gathers the dark long before the sunset colour has faded from the flattened sky, and one may then walk there in the peace of the earth gloom and hear from far below the great reverberation of the sea.

West of this treeless waste the Nauset Road mounts to.the upland floor of the Cape and to the inhabited lands.

When Henry Thoreau walked through Eastham in 1849, warding off a drenching autumnal rain with his Concord umbrella, he found this region practically treeless, and the inhabitants gathering their firewood on the beach. Nowadays, people on the outer Cape have their wood lots as well as inlanders. The tree that has rooted itself into the wind-swept bar is the pitch pine, *Pinus rigida*, the familiar tree of the outer Long Island wastes and the Jersey barrens. *Rigida* has no particular interest or beauty—one writer on trees calls it "rough and scraggly"—yet let me say no harm of it, for it is of value here: it furnishes firewood, holds down the earth and sand, and shelters the ploughed fields. In favourable situations, the pine reaches a height of between forty and fifty feet; on these windy sands, trees of the oldest growth struggle to reach between twenty-five and thirty. The trunk of this pine is brownish, with an overtone of violet, and seldom grows straight to its top; its leaves occur in a cluster of three, and its dry cones have a way of adhering for years to its branches.

They are forever burning up, these pitch-pine woods. A recent great fire in Wellfleet burned four days, and at one time seemed about to descend upon the town. Coast guard crews were sent to help the villagers. Many deer, they tell me, were seen running about in the burning woods, terror-stricken by the smoke and the oncoming crackle of the crest of flame. Encircled by the fire, one man jumped into a pond; scarce had he plunged when he heard a plunge close by and found a deer swimming by his side.

The thickets were rusty yesterday, for the tree thins out its winter-worn foliage in the spring. As I paused to study a group of particularly dead-looking trees, I scared up a large bird from the wood north of the road; it was a marsh hawk, *Circus Hudsonius.* Out of the withered tops flew this shape of warm, living brown, flapped, sailed on, and sank in the thickets by the marsh. I was glad to see this bird and to have some hint of its residence, because a female bird of this species makes a regular daily visit to the dunes. She comes from somewhere on the mainland north of the marsh, crosses the northeast corner of the flats, and on reaching the dunes aligns her flight with the long five miles of the great wall. Down the wall she comes, this great brown bird, flying fifteen or twenty feet above the awakening green. Now she hovers a second as if about to swoop, now she sinks as if about to snatch a prey—and all the time advancing. I have seen her flutter by the west windows of the Fo'castle so near that I could have touched her with a stick. Apparently, she is on the watch for beach mice, though I have as yet seen no mouse tracks on the dunes. She arrives between ten and eleven o'clock on practically all fair weather mornings, and occasionally I see her search the dunes again late in the afternoon. *Circus Hudsonius* is a migrant, but some birds spend the winter in southern New England, and I have a notion that this female has wintered in Nauset woods.

Once Nauset road approaches Eastham village the thickets of pitch pines to the eastward fall behind, the fields south of the road widen into superb treeless moorlands rolling down to the shores of the great lagoon, orchard tops become visible in hollows, and a few houses sit upon the moors like stranded ships. Eastham village itself, however, is not treeless, for there are shade trees near many houses and trees along the road.

All trees on the outer Cape are of interest to me, for they are the outermost of trees—trees with the roar of breakers in their leaves—but I find one group of especial interest. As one goes south along the main highway, one encounters a straggle of authentic western cottonwoods, *Populus deltoides*. The tree is rare in the northeast; indeed, these trees are the only ones of their kind I have ever chanced to find in Massachusetts. They were planted long ago, the village declares, by Cape Codders who emigrated to Kansas, and then returned, homesick for the sea. The trees grow close by the roadside, and there is a particularly fine group at the turn of the road near Mr. Austin Cole's. In this part of the Cape, an aërial fungus paints the trunks of deciduous trees an odd mustard-orange, and as I passed yesterday by the cottonwoods I saw that the group was particularly overspread with this picturesque stain. The growth seems to do no harm of any kind.

At a boulder commemorative of the men of Eastham who served in the Great War, I turned south on the main highway and presently reached the town hall and the western top of the moorland country. There I left the road and walked east into the moors to enjoy the incomparable view of the great Eastham marshes and the dunes. Viewed from the seaward scarp of the moors, the marsh takes form as the greener floor of a great encirclement of rolling, tawny, and treeless land. From a marsh just below, the vast flat islands and winding rivers of the marsh run level to the yellow bulwark of the dunes, and at the end of the vista the eye escapes through valleys in the wall to the cold April blue of the North Atlantic plain. The floor of ocean there seems higher than the floor of the marsh, and sailing vessels often have an air of sailing past the dunes low along the sky. A faint green colours the sky line of the dunes, and on the wide flanks of the empty moorlands stains of springtime greenness well from the old tawniness of earth. Yesterday I heard no ocean sound.

So beautiful was the spacious and elemental scene that I lingered a while on the top of the moor cliff shelving to the marsh. The tide was rising in the creeks and channels, and the gulls remaining in the region had been floated off their banks and shoals. The great levels seemed, for the moment, empty of their winged and silvery life.

During the winter, one bird has made this moorland region all his own, and that bird the English starling. The birds apparently spend the winter on these hills. I have crossed the open country during a northeast gale just to watch them wheeling in the snow. Scarce had one flock settled ere another was up; I saw them here and there and far away. I find these Eastham birds of particular interest, for they are the first American starlings I have seen to recover their ancestral and European mode of life. In Europe, the bird is given to congregating in vast flocks— there are river lowlands in England where such starling flocks gather in crowded thousands— and once this starling army has established itself in a region it is theirs completely and forever.

Are the flocks at Eastham the beginning of one of those European mobs? Will the various flocks now inhabiting the moors ultimately mingle to form one enormous and tyrannous confederacy? The separate winter swarms already consist of fifty to seventy-five birds, and I imagine that, if the stray members of each flock were to return to their congregations, these bands might be found to contain well over a hundred individuals. Such a mingling as I speak of may possibly take place; again, it may be that the resources of the region are already taxed to support the present birds; let us hope that this last is the truth. The presence of these rabble blackbirds disturbs the entire natural economy of the region, for they strip every autumnal bush and plant bare of its last seed and berry and leave nothing for our native birds to feed on when they return in the spring.

With spring, the birds desert the moors, pair off, and retire to the village barns and the chimneys of unopened summer cottages.

The hour of flood tide approaching, I left the moors behind and went to the west shore to see what I could of the strangest of all regional migrations.

III

Some five years ago, on a night in early April, I happened to be aboard a United States naval vessel bound coastwise from the southern dril!

grounds to New York. Our course lay well out of sight of land; the night was springlike, still and mild, the stars thick-sown in a faintly hazy sky. I remember that we saw the lights of a few ships standing in to Philadelphia. Once these had dimmed and disappeared behind, the sea was entirely our own, a vast, lonely, still, and starlit sea. Just after one o'clock I saw ahead of us on the sea a field, a shimmer of pale light, formless as the reflection of a cloud and mysteriously troubled by auroral undulations. We had overtaken a migration of fish moving north along the coast with the advance of spring. The skirts of the sun's robe, trailing over ocean, stir the deep, and its mysterious peoples move North on the fringes of the light. I do not know what species of fish I chanced that night to see, for there is a definite and populous area of marine life lying between Hatteras and Cape Cod. They may possibly have been herring. As our vessel neared the living shoal, it seemed to move as one thing, there coursed through it a new vibration, and it turned east, grew vague, and vanished completely in the night.

Every spring even such a fish migration, moving through ocean as mysteriously as the force of a wave, breaks against our south New England shore. In colonial times the younger Winthrop wrote of it, telling of "the coming up of a fish called aloofes into the rivers. Where the ground is bad or worn out, the Indians used to put two or three of the forementioned fishes under or adjacent each corn hill. The English have learned like husbandry where those aloofes come up in great plenty." This "alooofe" of the colonists, better known as the "alewife," and often and incorrectly called a "herring," is really not a herring at all but a related fish, *Pomolobus pseudo-harengus*. It is distinguishable from the true sea herring by its greater depth of body and by the serrations on the midline of its belly which are stronger and sharper than those of the true herring—so sharp, indeed, that the fish is sometimes called a "saw belly." In April they leave the sea and run up our brooks to spawn in fresh-water ponds.

There is a famous brook in Weymouth, Massachusetts, which I try to visit every year. I remember the last warm April day. The "herring" brook—it is scarce more than ten or twelve feet wide and hardly more than a foot deep—was flowing freely, its clear brownish waters rippling almost noiselessly in the morning light. The fish were "in," moving up the brook as thickly massed as a battalion along a narrow road; there were no ranks—only an onward swarming. So numerous were the fish, and so regimented, that I stopped at the water's edge and easily caught two or three with my bare hand. Through the brownish stream the eye looked down to numberless long backs of a subdued dark lavender-grey and to a fleet of dorsal fins breaking water. The brook smelt of fish. Here and there were dead ones, aground on the edges of the stream or held by the current against a rock; dead things lying on their sides, with opaque, slime-coated eyes, and rock bruises on their sides—raw spots of fish blood red in a side of brown and golden scales. Sometimes the advance seemed stilled till the studying eye perceived the constant individual advance. A hundred thousand had come.

These alewives of Weymouth come up out of the sea, and from Heaven knows just where out of the sea. They run up Weymouth Brook, are stopped by a dam, are fished out in a net, dumped into barrels of water, and carted overland in a truck to Whitman's Pond. I have watched them follow currents in the pond, once they have been spilled out into it. Then comes, perhaps, a sense of arrival and intended time; each female lays from sixty thousand to a hundred thousand glutinous eggs, these drop to the bottom, drift along the mud, and ooze and attach themselves as chance directs. The spawning females and the males then go over the dam and back to sea, the herring born in the pond follow them ten months or a year later, and then comes another spring and a great mystery. Somewhere in the depths of ocean, each Weymouth-born fish remembers Whitman's Pond, and comes to it through the directionless leagues of the sea. What stirs in each cold brain? what call quivers as the new sun strikes down into the river of ocean? how do the creatures find their way? Birds have landscape and rivers and headlands of the coast, the fish have—what? But presently the fish are "in" at Weymouth, breasting the brook's spring overflow to the ancestral pond.

Some remember Whitman's Pond, others remember the ponds of the Cape. There are "herring" ponds and "herring" brooks on the map of Eastham.

The road to the bay leads off at the town hall,

passing an old windmill which still has its grinding machinery in place. I entered it once, long ago, to see the dusty chutes, the empty bins, and the stones in their cheese-box cases of ancient and mellow wood. Locust trees inclose it, and song sparrows perch on the arms that have not turned for years. I heard one as I trod the dusty floor, his mating song entering through a broken pane. Beyond the mill, the road passes a scatter of houses, crosses the railroad track, winds between the ponds of Eastham, and then comes to an open mile of sandy fields and pitch-pine country extending to the bay.

The road descends, for the bay rim of the outer Cape is lower than the ocean wall. North of the road, it is but a bank at the end of fields. Accustomed to the roar of the ocean beach and to the salt wind in my ears, the quiet of the bay fell strangely about me. There was no surf, scarce a lakelike ripple; masses of weed, shaped in long undulations by water waves, lay heavy on the beach; forty miles across, earth-blue beyond blue water, and mounded and separate as so many isles, appeared the highlands of Plymouth woods and Sagamore. A few ducks were feeding more than a mile offshore, and, as I watched, a solitary drake rose from the broad marshes to my right and flew off to join them.

The quiet of the bay, the subdued easterly blowing across the fields, the belt of winter weed, the glint and warmth of the sun, the solitary bird—there was a sense of old times dead and of new times beginning—recurrence, life, the turn of the sun's wheel, always the imperative, bright sun.

I walked along the beach to the mouth of the "herring" brook. The stream is but a clogged gully of clean water running down to the sea through the sandy open meadows. Arriving at the shore, it spills out over the beach and trickles down to the bay. Low tides wash at the trickling rills and cover them; high tides climb the beach and enter a pool which has formed at the mouth behind a dam of weed. Yesterday, the low course tide had scarce touched the edge of the barrier and had begun to ebb an hour before my coming. Between the dam and the high-tide mark of the day lay a twenty-foot interval of beach traced by flat rillets seeping from the barrier. I looked into the pool. The "herring" had been in, for there was a dead one lying on the bottom of weed, a golden fish silted over with fine mud.

Suddenly, on chancing to look bay-ward, I saw a small school of "herring" just off the mouth of the brook and scarce more than fifteen feet from the motionless rim of the tide. There were, perhaps, fifty or a hundred fish in the school. Occasional fins chopped the quiet water. "Herrings" of Eastham brook unable to enter the pond in which they were born, barred from it by a dam of Nature's making. As I stood looking off to the baffled creatures, now huddled and seemingly still in deeper water, now huddled and all astir in the shallowest fringes of the tide, I began to reflect on Nature's eagerness to sow life everywhere, to fill the planet with it, to crowd with it the earth, the air, and the seas. Into every empty corner, into all forgotten things and nooks, Nature struggles to pour life, pouring life into the dead, life into life itself. That immense, overwhelming, relentless, burning ardency of Nature for the stir of life! And all these her creatures, even as these thwarted lives, what travail, what hunger and cold, what bruising and slow-killing struggle will they not endure to accomplish the earth's purpose? and what conscious resolution of men can equal their impersonal, their congregate will to yield self life to the will of life universal?

The tide ebbed, swiftly shallowing over the flats, the "herring" vanished from sight like a reflection from a glass; I could not tell when they were gone or the manner of their going.

Returning to the outer beach late in the afternoon, I found the ocean all a cold jade-green sown with whitecaps, the wind rising, and great broken clouds flowing over from the east. And in this northern current was a new warmth.

Chapter VIII

NIGHT ON THE GREAT BEACH

I

Our fantastic civilization has fallen out of touch with many aspects of nature, and with none more completely than with night. Primitive folk, gathered at a cave mouth round a fire, do not fear night; they fear, rather, the energies and creatures to whom night gives power; we of the age of the machines, having delivered ourselves of nocturnal enemies, now have a dislike of night itself. With lights and ever more lights, we drive the holiness and beauty of night back to the forests and the sea; the little villages, the crossroads even, will have none of it. Are modern folk, perhaps, afraid of night? Do they fear that vast serenity, the mystery of infinite space, the austerity of stars? Having made themselves at home in a civilization obsessed with power, which explains its whole world in terms of energy, do they fear at night for their dull acquiescence and the pattern of their beliefs? Be the answer what it will, to-day's civilization is full of people who have not the slightest notion of the character or the poetry of night, who have never even seen night. Yet to live thus, to know only artificial night, is as absurd and evil as to know only artificial day.

Night is very beautiful on this great beach. It is the true other half of the day's tremendous wheel; no lights without meaning stab or trouble it; it is beauty, it is fulfilment, it is rest. Thin clouds float in these heavens, islands of obscurity in a splendour of space and stars: the Milky Way bridges earth and ocean; the beach resolves itself into a unity of form, its summer lagoons, its slopes and uplands merging; against the western sky and the falling bow of sun rise the silent and superb undulations of the dunes.

My nights are at their darkest when a dense fog streams in from the sea under a black, unbroken floor of cloud. Such nights are rare, but are most to be expected when fog gathers off the coast in early summer; this last Wednesday night was the darkest I have known. Between ten o'clock and two in the morning three vessels stranded on the outer beach—a fisherman, a four-masted schooner, and a beam trawler. The fisherman and the schooner have been towed off, but the trawler, they say, is still ashore.

I went down to the beach that night just after ten o'clock. So utterly black, pitch dark it was, and so thick with moisture and trailing showers, that there was no sign whatever of the beam of Nauset; the sea was only a sound, and when I reached the edge of the surf the dunes themselves had disappeared behind. I stood as isolate in that immensity of rain and night as I might have stood in interplanetary space. The sea was troubled and noisy, and when I opened the darkness with an outlined cone of light from my electric torch I saw that the waves were washing up green coils of sea grass, all coldly wet and bright in the motionless and unnatural radiance. Far off a single ship was groaning its way along the shoals. The fog was compact of the finest moisture; passing by, it spun itself into my lens of light like a kind of strange, aërial, and liquid silk. Effin Chalke, the new coast guard, passed me going north, and told me that he had had news at the halfway house of the schooner at Cahoon's.

It was dark, pitch dark to my eye, yet complete darkness, I imagine, is exceedingly rare, perhaps unknown in outer nature. The nearest natural approximation to it is probably the gloom of forest country buried in night and cloud. Dark as the night was here, there was still light on the surface of the planet. Standing on the shelving beach, with the surf breaking at my feet, I could see the endless wild uprush, slide, and withdrawal of the sea's white rim of foam. The men at Nauset tell me that on such nights they follow along this vague crawl of whiteness, trusting to habit and a sixth sense to warn them of their approach to the halfway house.

Animals descend by starlight to the beach. North, beyond the dunes, muskrats forsake the cliff and nose about in the driftwood and weed, leaving intricate trails and figure eights to be obliterated by the day; the lesser folk—the mice, the occasional small sand-coloured toads, the burrowing moles—keep to the upper beach and leave their tiny footprints under the overhanging wall. In autumn skunks, beset by a shrinking larder, go beach combing early in the night. The animal is by preference a clean feeder and turns up his nose at rankness. I almost stepped on a big fellow one night as I was walking north to meet the first man south from Nauset. There was a scamper, and the creature ran up the beach from under my feet; alarmed he certainly was, yet was he contained and continent. Deer are frequently seen, especially north of the light. I find their tracks upon the summer dunes.

Years ago, while camping on this beach north of Nauset, I went for a stroll along the top of the cliff at break of dawn. Though the path followed close enough along the edge, the beach below was often hidden, and I looked directly from the height to the flush of sunrise at sea. Presently the path, turning, approached the brink of the earth precipice, and on the beach below, in the cool, wet rosiness of dawn, I saw three deer playing. They frolicked, rose on their hind legs, scampered off, and returned again, and were merry. Just before sunrise they trotted off north together down the beach toward a hollow in the cliff and the path that climbs it.

Occasionally a sea creature visits the shore at night. Lone coast guardsmen, trudging the sand at some deserted hour, have been startled by seals. One man fell flat on a creature's back, and it drew away from under him, flippering toward the sea, with a sound "halfway between a squeal and a bark." I myself once had rather a start. It was long after sundown, the light dying and uncertain, and I was walking home on the top level of the beach and close along the slope descending to the ebbing tide. A little more than halfway to the Fo'castle a huge unexpected something suddenly writhed horribly in the darkness under my bare foot. I had stepped on a skate left stranded by some recent crest of surf, and my weight had momentarily annoyed it back to life.

Facing north, the beam of Nauset becomes part of the dune night. As I walk toward it, I see the lantern, now as a star of light which waxes and wanes three mathematic times, now as a lovely pale flare of light behind the rounded summits of the dunes. The changes in the atmosphere change the colour of the beam; it is now whitish, now flame golden, now golden red; it changes its form as well, from a star to a blare of light, from a blare of light to a cone of radiance sweeping a circumference of fog. To the west of Nauset I often see the apocalyptic flash of the great light at the Highland reflected on the clouds or even on the moisture in the starlit air, and, seeing it, I often think of the pleasant hours I have spent there when George and Mary Smith were at the light and I had the good fortune to visit as their guest. Instead of going to sleep in the room under the eaves, I would lie awake, looking out of a window to the great spokes of light revolving as solemnly as a part of the universe.

All night long the lights of coastwise vessels pass at sea, green lights going south, red lights moving north. Fishing schooners and flounder draggers anchor two or three miles out, and keep a bright riding light burning on the mast. I see them come to anchor at sundown, but I rarely see them go, for they are off at dawn. When busy at night, these fishermen illumine their decks with a scatter of oil flares. From shore, the ships might be thought afire. I have watched the scene through a night glass. I could see no smoke, only the waving flares, the reddish radiance on sail and rigging, an edge of reflection overside, and the enormous night and sea beyond.

One July night, as I returned at three o'clock from an expedition north, the whole night, in one strange, burning instant, turned into a phantom day. I stopped and, questioning, stared about. An enormous meteor, the largest I have ever seen, was consuming itself in an effulgence of light west of the zenith. Beach and dune and ocean appeared out of nothing, shadowless and motionless, a landscape whose every tremor and vibration were stilled, a landscape in a dream.

The beach at night has a voice all its own, a sound in fullest harmony with its spirit and mood —with its little, dry noise of sand forever moving, with its solemn, overspilling, rhythmic seas, with its eternity of stars that sometimes seem to hang down like lamps from the high heavens— and that sound the piping of a bird. As I walk the beach in early summer my solitary coming disturbs it on its nest, and it flies away, troubled, invisible, piping its sweet, plaintive cry. The bird I write of is the piping plover, *Charadrius melodus*, sometimes called the beach plover or the mourning bird. Its note is a whistled syllable, the loveliest musical note, I think, sounded by any North Atlantic bird.

Now that summer is here I often cook myself a camp supper on the beach. Beyond the crackling, salt-yellow driftwood flame, over the pyramid of barrel staves, broken boards, and old sticks all atwist with climbing fire, the unseen ocean thunders and booms, the breaker sounding hollow as it falls. The wall of the sand cliff behind, with its rim of grass and withering roots, its sandy crumblings and erosions, stands gilded with flame; wind cries over it; a covey of sand-pipers pass between the ocean and the fire. There are stars, and to the south Scorpio hangs curving down the sky with ringed Saturn shining in his claw.

Learn to reverence night and to put away the vulgar fear of it, for, with the banishment of night from the experience of man, there vanishes as well a religious emotion, a poetic mood, which gives depth to the adventure of humanity. By day, space is one with the earth and with man— it is his sun that is shining, his clouds that are floating past; at night, space is his no more. When the great earth, abandoning day, rolls up the deeps of the heavens and the universe, a new door opens for the human spirit, and there are few so clownish that some awareness of the mystery of being does not touch them as they gaze. For a moment of night we have a glimpse of ourselves and of our world islanded in its stream of stars—pilgrims of mortality, voyaging between horizons across eternal seas of space and time. Fugitive though the instant be, the spirit of man is, during it, ennobled by a genuine moment of emotional dignity, and poetry makes its own both the human spirit and experience.

II

At intervals during the summer, often enough when the tides are high and the moon is near the full, the surf along the beach turns from a churn of empty moonlit water to a mass of panic life. Driven in by schools of larger fish, swarms of little fish enter the tumble of the surf, the eaters follow them, the surf catches them both up and throws them, mauled and confused, ashore.

Under a sailing moon, the whole churn of sea close off the beach vibrates with a primeval ferocity and intensity of life; yet is this war of rushing mouth and living food without a sound save for the breaking of the seas. But let me tell of such a night.

I had spent an afternoon ashore with friends, and they had driven me to Nauset Station just after nine o'clock. The moon, two days from the full, was very lovely on the moors and on the channels and flat, moon-green isles of the lagoon; the wind was southerly and light. Moved by its own enormous rhythms, the surf that night was a stately incoming of high, serried waves, the last wave alone breaking. This inmost wave broke heavily in a smother and rebound of sandy foam, and thin sheets of seethe, racing before it up the beach, vanished endlessly into the endless thirst of the sands. As I neared the surf rim to begin my walk to the southward, I saw that the beach close along the breakers, as far as the eye would reach, was curiously atwinkle in the moonlight with the convulsive dance of myriads of tiny fish. The breakers were spilling them on the sands; the surf was aswarm with the creatures; it was indeed, for the time being, a surf of life. And this surf of life was breaking for miles along the Cape.

Little herring or mackerel? Sand eels? I picked a dancer out of the slide and held him up to the moon. It was the familiar sand eel or sand launce, *Ammodytes americanus*, of the waters between Hatteras and Labrador. This is no kin of the true eels, though he rather resembles one in general appearance, for his body is slender, eel-like, and round. Instead of ending bluntly, however, this "eel" has a large, well-forked tail. The fish in the surf were two and three inches long.

Homeward that night I walked barefooted in the surf, watching the convulsive, twinkling dance, now and then feeling the squirm of a fish across my toes. Presently something occurred which made me keep to the thinnest edge of the foam. Some ten feet ahead, an enormous dogfish was suddenly borne up the beach on the rim of a slide of foam; he moved with it unresisting while it carried him; the slide withdrawing and drying up, it rolled him twice over seaward; he then twisted heavily, and another minor slide carried him back again to shore. The fish was about three feet long, a real junior shark, purplish black in the increasing light—for the moon was moving west across the long axis of the breakers —and his dark, important bulk seemed strange in the bright dance of the smaller fish about him.

It was then that I began to look carefully at the width of gathering seas. Here were the greater fish, the mouths, the eaters who had driven the "eels" ashore to the edge of their world and into ours. The surf was alive with dogfish, aswarm with them, with the rush, the cold bellies, the twist and tear of their wolfish violence of life. Yet there was but little sign of it in the waters— a rare fin slicing past, and once the odd and instant glimpse of a fish embedded like a fly in amber in the bright, overturning volute of a wave.

Too far in, the dogfish were now in the grip of the surf, and presently began to come ashore. As I walked the next half mile every other breaker seemed to leave behind its ebb a mauled and stranded sharklet feebly sculling with his tail. I kicked many back into the seas, risking a toe, perhaps; some I caught by the tails and flung, for I did not want them corrupting on the beach. The next morning, in the mile and three quarters between the Fo'castle and the station, I counted seventy-one dogfish lying dead on the upper beach. There were also a dozen or two skates—the skate is really a kind of shark— which had stranded the same night. Skates follow in many things, and are forever being flung upon these sands.

I sat up late that night at the Fo'castle, often putting down the book I read to return to the beach.

A little after eleven came Bill Eldredge to the door, with a grin on his face and one hand held behind his back. "Have you ordered to-morrow's dinner yet?" said he. "No." "Well, here it is," and Bill produced a fine cod from behind his back. "Just found him right in front of your door, alive and flopping. Yes, yes, haddock and cod often chase those sand eels in with the bigger fish; often find them on the beach about this time of the year. Got any place to keep him?

Let me have a piece of string and I'll hang him on your clothesline. He'll keep all right." With a deft unforking of two fingers, Bill drew the line through the gills, and as he did so the heavy fish flopped noisily. No fear about him being dead. Make a nice chowder. Bill stepped outside; I heard him at the clothesline. Afterward we talked till it was time for him to shoulder his clock and Coston case again, pick up his watch cap, whistle in his little black dog, and go down over the dune to the beach and Nauset Station.

There were nights in June when there was phosphorescence in the surf and on the beach, and one such night I think I shall remember as the most strange and beautiful of all the year.

Early this summer the middle beach moulded itself into a bar, and between it and the dunes are long, shallow runnels into which the ocean spills over at high tide. On the night I write of, the first quarter of the moon hung in the west, and its light on the sheets of incoming tide coursing thin across the bar was very beautiful to see. Just after sundown I walked to Nauset with friends who had been with me during the afternoon; the tide was still rising, and a current running in the pools. I lingered at the station with my friends till the last of sunset had died, and the light upon the planet, which had been moonlight mingled with sunset pink, had cleared to pure cold moon.

Southward, then, I turned, and because the flooded runnels were deep close by the station, I could not cross them and had to walk their inner shores. The tide had fallen half a foot, perhaps, but the breakers were still leaping up against the bar as against a wall, the greater ones still spilling over sheets of vanishing foam.

It grew darker with the westing of the moon. There was light on the western tops of the dunes, a fainter light on the lower beach and the breakers; the face of the dunes was a unity of dusk.

The tide had ebbed in the pools, and their edges were wet and dark. There was a strange contrast between the still levels of the pool and the seethe of the sea. I kept close to the land edge of the lagoons, and as I advanced my boots kicked wet spatters of sand ahead as they might have kicked particles of snow. Every spatter was a crumb of phosphorescence; I walked in a dust of stars. Behind me, in my footprints, luminous patches burned. With the double-ebb moonlight and tide, the deepening brims of the pools took shape in smouldering, wet fire. So strangely did the luminous speckles smoulder and die and glow that it seemed as if some wind were passing, by whose breath they were kindled and extinguished. Occasional whole breakers of phosphorescence rolled in out of the vague sea—the whole wave one ghostly motion, one creamy light—and, breaking against the bar, flung up pale sprays of fire.

A strange thing happens here during these luminous tides. The phosphorescence is itself a mass of life, sometimes protozoan its origin, sometimes bacterial, the phosphorescence I write of being probably the latter. Once this living light has seeped into the beach, colonies of it speedily invade the tissues of the ten thousand thousand sand fleas which are forever hopping on this edge of ocean. Within an hour the grey bodies of these swarming amphipods, these useful, ever hungry sea scavengers (*Orchestia agilis; Talorchestia megalophthalma*), show phosphorescent pin points, and these points grow and unite till the whole creature is luminous. The attack is really a disease, an infection of light. The process had already begun when I arrived on the beach on the night of which I am writing, and the luminous

fleas hopping off before my boots were an extraordinary sight. It was curious to see them hop
from the pool rims to the upper beach, paling
as they reached the width of peaceful moonlight
lying landward of the strange, crawling beauty
of the pools. This infection kills them, I think;
at least, I have often found the larger creature
lying dead on the fringe of the beach, his huge
porcelain eyes and water-grey body one core of
living fire. Round and about him, disregarding,
ten thousand kinsmen, carrying on life and the
plan of life, ate of the bounty of the tide.

III

All winter long I slept on a couch in my larger
room, but with the coming of warm weather I
have put my bedroom in order—I used it as a
kind of storage space during the cold season—
and returned to my old and rather rusty iron
cot. Every once in a while, however, moved by
some obscure mood, I lift off the bedclothing and
make up the couch again for a few nights. I like
the seven windows of the larger room, and the
sense one may have there of being almost out-
of-doors. My couch stands alongside the two
front windows, and from my pillow I can look

out to sea and watch the passing lights, the stars rising over ocean, the swaying lanterns of the anchored fishermen, and the white spill of the surf whose long sound fills the quiet of the dunes.

Ever since my coming I have wanted to see a thunderstorm bear down upon this elemental coast. A thunderstorm is a "tempest" on the Cape. The quoted word, as Shakespeare used it, means lightning and thunder, and it is in this old and beautiful Elizabethan sense that the word is used in Eastham. When a schoolboy in the Orleans or the Wellfleet High reads the Shakespearean play, its title means to him exactly what it meant to the man from Stratford; elsewhere in America, the terms seems to mean anything from a tornado to a blizzard. I imagine that this old significance of the word is now to be found only in certain parts of England and Cape Cod.

On the night of the June tempest, I was sleeping in my larger room, the windows were open, and the first low roll of thunder opened my eyes. It had been very still when I went to bed, but now a wind from the west-nor'west was blowing through the windows in a strong and steady current, and as I closed them there was lightning to the west and far away. I looked at my watch;

it was just after one o'clock. Then came a time of waiting in the darkness, long minutes broken by more thunder, and intervals of quiet in which I heard a faintest sound of light surf upon the beach. Suddenly the heavens cracked open in an immense instant of pinkish-violet lightning. My seven windows filled with the violent, inhuman light, **and I** had a glimpse of the great, solitary dunes staringly empty of familiar shadows; a tremendous crash then mingled with the withdrawal of the light, and echoes of thunder rumbled away and grew faint in a returning rush of darkness. A moment after, rain began to fall gently as if someone had just released its flow, a blessed sound on a roof of wooden shingles, and one I have loved ever since I was a child. From a gentle patter the sound of the rain grew swiftly to a drumming roar, and with the rain came the chuckling of water from the eaves. The tempest was crossing the Cape, striking at the ancient land on its way to the heavens above the sea.

Now came flash after stabbing flash amid a roaring of rain, and heavy thunder that rolled on till its last echoes were swallowed up in vast detonations which jarred the walls. Houses were struck that night in Eastham village. My lonely world, full of lightning and rain, was strange to look upon. I do not share the usual fear of lightning, but that night there came over me, for the first and last time of all my solitary year, a sense of isolation and remoteness from my kind. I remember that I stood up, watching, in the middle of the room. On the great marshes the lightning surfaced the winding channels with a metallic splendour and arrest of motion, all very strange through windows blurred by rain. Under the violences of light the great dunes took on a kind of elemental passivity, the quiet of earth enchanted into stone, and as I watched them appear and plunge back into a darkness that had an intensity of its own I felt, as never before, a sense of the vast time, of the thousands of cyclic and uncounted years which had passed since these giants had risen from the dark ocean at their feet and given themselves to the wind and the bright day.

Fantastic things were visible at sea. Beaten down by the rain, and sheltered by the Cape itself from the river of west wind, the offshore brim of ocean remained unusually calm. The tide was about halfway up the beach, and rising, and long parallels of low waves, forming close inshore, were curling over and breaking placidly along the lonely, rain-drenched miles. The intense crackling flares and quiverings of the storm, moving out to sea, illumined every inch of the beach and the plain of the Atlantic, all save the hollow bellies of the little breakers, which were shielded from the light by their overcurling crests. The effect was dramatic and strangely beautiful, for what one saw was a bright ocean rimmed with parallel bands of blackest advancing darkness, each one melting back to light as the wave toppled down upon the beach in foam.

Stars came out after the storm, and when I woke again before sunrise I found the heavens and the earth rainwashed, cool, and clear. Saturn and the Scorpion were setting, but Jupiter was riding the zenith and paling on his throne. The tide was low in the marsh channels; the gulls had scarcely stirred upon their gravel banks and bars. Suddenly, thus wandering about, I disturbed a song sparrow on her nest. She flew to the roof of my house, grasped the ridgepole, and turned about, apprehensive, inquiring . . . *'tsiped* her monosyllable of alarm. Then back toward her nest she flew, alighted in a plum bush, and, reassured at last, trilled out a morning song.

Chapter IX

THE YEAR AT HIGH TIDE

I

Had I room in this book, I should like to write a whole chapter on the sense of smell, for all my life long I have had of that sense an individual enjoyment. To my mind, we live too completely by the eye. I like a good smell—the smell of a freshly ploughed field on a warm morning after a night of April rain, the clovelike aroma of our wild Cape Cod pinks, the morning perfume of lilacs showery with dew, the good reek of hot salt grass and low tide blowing from these meadows late on summer afternoons.

What a stench modern civilization breathes, and how have we ever learned to endure that foul blue air? In the Seventeenth Century, the air about a city must have been much the same air as overhung a large village; to-day the town atmosphere is to be endured only by the new synthetic man.

Our whole English tradition neglects smell. In English, the nose is still something of an indelicate organ, and I am not so sure that its use is not regarded as somewhat sensual. Our literary pictures, our poetic landscapes are things to hang on the mind's wall, things for the eye. French letters are more indulgent to the nose; one can scarcely read ten lines of any French verse without encountering the omnipresent, the inevitable *parfum*. And here the French are right, for though the eye is the human master sense and chief æsthetic gate, the creation of a mood or of a moment of earth poetry is a rite for which other senses may be properly invoked. Of all such appeals to sensory recollection, none are more powerful, none open a wider door in the brain than an appeal to the nose. It is a sense that every lover of the elemental world ought to use, and, using, enjoy. We ought to keep all senses vibrant and alive. Had we done so, we should never have built a civilization which outrages them, which so outrages them, indeed, that a vicious circle has been established and the dull sense grown duller.

One reason for my love of this great beach is that, living here, I dwell in a world that has a good natural smell, that is full of keen, vivid, and interesting savours and fragrances. I have them at their best, perhaps, when hot days are dulled with a warm rain. So well do I know them, indeed, that were I blindfolded and led about the summer beach, I think I could tell on what part of it I was at any moment standing. At the ocean's very edge the air is almost always cool—cold even—and delicately moist with surf spray and the endless dissolution of the innumerable bubbles of the foam slides; the wet sand slope beneath exhales a cool savour of mingling beach and sea, and the innermost breakers push ahead of them puffs of this fragrant air. It is a singular experience to walk this brim of ocean when the wind is blowing almost directly down the beach, but now veering a point toward the dunes, now a point toward the sea. For twenty feet a humid and tropical exhalation of hot, wet sand encircles one, and from this one steps, as through a door, into as many yards of mid-September. In a point of time, one goes from Central America to Maine.

Atop the broad eight-foot back of the summer bar, inland forty feet or so from the edge of low tide, other odours wait. Here have the tides strewn a moist tableland with lumpy tangles,

wisps, and matted festoons of ocean vegetation—
with common sea grass, with rockweed olive-
green and rockweed olive-brown, with the
crushed and wrinkled green leaves of sea lettuce,
with edible, purple-red dulse and bleached sea
moss, with slimy and gelatinous cords seven and
eight feet long. In the hot noontide they lie,
slowly, slowly withering—for their very substance is water—and sending an odour of ocean
and vegetation into the burning air. I like this
good natural savour. Sometimes a dead, surf-
trapped fish, perhaps a dead skate curling up in
the heat, adds to this odour of vegetation a faint
fishy rankness, but the smell is not earth corrup-
tion, and the scavengers of the beach soon enough
remove the cause.

Beyond the bar and the tidal runnel farther in,
the flat region I call the upper beach runs back
to the shadeless bastion of the dunes. In summer
this beach is rarely covered by the tides. Here
lies a hot and pleasant odour of sand. I find myself an angle of shade slanting off from a mass
of wreckage still embedded in a dune, take up
a handful of the dry, bright sand, sift it slowly
through my fingers, and note how the heat brings
out the fine, sharp, stony smell of it. There is weed

here, too, well buried in the dry sand—flotsam of last month's high, full-moon tides. In the shadowless glare, the topmost fronds and heart-shaped air sacs have ripened to an odd iodine orange and a blackish iodine brown. Overwhelmed thus by sand and heat, the aroma of this foliage has dissolved; only a shower will summon it again from these crisping, strangely coloured leaves.

Cool breath of eastern ocean, the aroma of beach vegetation in the sun, the hot, pungent exhalation of fine sand—these mingled are the midsummer savour of the beach.

II

In my open, treeless world, the year is at flood tide. All day long and all night long, for four days and five days, the southwest wind blows across the Cape with the tireless constancy of a planetary river. The sun, descending the altar of the year, pauses ritually on the steps of the summer months, the disk of flame overflowing. On hot days the beach is tremulous with rising, visible heat bent seaward by the wind; a blue haze hangs inland over the moors and the great marsh blotting out pictorial individualities and reducing the landscape to a mass. Dune days are sometimes hotter than village days, for the naked glare of sand reflects the heat; dune nights are always cooler. On its sun-trodden sand, between the marsh wind and the coolness of ocean, the Fo'castle has been as comfortable as a ship at sea.

The duneland air burns with the smell of sand, ocean, and sun. On the tops of the hills, the grass stands at its tallest and greenest, its new straw-green seed plumes rising through a dead crop of last year's withered spears. On some leaves there is already a tiny spot of orange wither at the very tip, and thin lines of wither descending on either edge. Grasses in the salt meadows are fruiting; there are brownish and greenish-yellow patches on the levels of summer green. On the dunes, the sand lies quiescent in a tangle of grass; in naked places, it lies as if it were held down by the sun. When there has been no rain for a week or more, and the slanting flame has been heavy on the beach, the sand in my path down Fo'castle dune becomes so dry, so loose and deep, that I trudge through it as through snow.

The winter sea was a mirror in a cold, half-lighted room, the summer sea is a mirror in a room burning with light. So abundant is the light and so huge the mirror that the whole of a summer day floats reflected on the glass. Colours gather there, sunrise and twilight, cloud shadows and cloud reflections, the pewter dullness of gathering rain, the blue, burning splendour of space swept free of every cloud. Light transfixes ocean, and some warmth steals in with the light, but the waves that glint in the sun are still a tingling cold.

Now do insects inherit the warm earth. When a sluggish wind blows from the marsh on a hot day, the dunes can be tropical. The sand quivers with insect lives. On such days, "greenheads," *Tabanus costalis*, stab and buzz, sand gnats or "no-see-ums" gather in myriads on the sun-drenched south wall of the house, "flatiron flies" and minor unknowns swarm to the attack. One must remain indoors or take a precarious refuge at the ocean's very edge. Thanks to the wind, the coolness, and the spray, the lower beach is usually free of insect bloodletters, though the bullying, poisonous Tabanid, in the mid-August height of his season, can be a hateful nuisance. So far, however, I have had but two of these tropical visitations. Barring an extra allowance of greenheads, the dunes are probably quite as habitable as any stretch of outermost beach. The wind, moreover, saves me from mosquitoes.

Ants have appeared, and the upper beach is pitted with their hills; I watch the tiny, red-brown creatures running in and out of buried weed. Just outside each hole, the fine sand is all delicately ascrawl with the small, endless comings and goings. The whole upper beach, indeed, has become a plain of intense and minute life; there are tunnels and doors and pitways everywhere. The dune locusts that were so small in June have grown large and learned to make a sound. All up and down the dunes, sometimes swept seaward out of their course by the west wind, go various butterflies. When I turn up driftwood in the dunes, or walk the wheel ruts in the meadows, crickets race off into the grass.

On the dunes, in open places near thin grass, I find the deep, finger-round mine shafts of the dune spider. A foot below, in the cooler sand, lives the black female; dig her up, and you will find a hairy, spidery ball. During the summer months the lady does not leave her cave, but in early autumn she revisits the world and scuttles through the dune grass, black, fast, and formidable. The smaller, sand-coloured male runs about everywhere. I saw one on the beach the other night, running along in cloudy moonlight, and mistook him at first for a small crab. Later the same night, I found a tiny, sand-coloured dune toad at the very brim of the surf, and wondered if an appetite for beach fleas had led him there.

"June bugs," *Lachnosterna arcuta*, strike my screens with a formidable boom and linger there formidably buzzing; let me but open the door, and half a dozen are tilting at my table lamp and falling stunned upon the cloth. On mounded slopes of sand, solitary black wasps scratch themselves out a cave; across my paths move the shadows of giant dragon flies.

The straggling beach peas of the region are in bloom; the west wind blows the grass and rushes out to the rippled levels of a level sea; heat clouds hang motionless on the land horizon, their lower rims lost in the general haze; the great sun overflows; the year burns on.

III

I have spoken in another chapter of the melting away of bird life from this region during April and May. There was a time when the all-the-year-round herring gulls seemed the only

birds left to me, and many of these were immature birds or birds whose plumage was then
changing from immature brown to adult white
and grey. One cold, foggy morning late in May,
I woke to find the beach in front of the Fo'castle
crowded with these gulls, for a number of hake
had stranded during the night, and the birds
had discovered them and come to feed. Some fed
on the fresh fish, findings being keepings—I saw
various birds defend their individual repasts
from late arrivals and would-be sharers with a
show of wings and a hostile cry—others stood
on the top of the beach in a long, senatorial row
facing the sea. The maturing birds were of all
tones of white and brown; some were chalky
and brown, some were speckled like hens, others
were a curious brown-mottled chalky grey.
The moults of herring gulls are complicated af-
fairs. There are spring moults and autumn
moults, partial moults and second nuptial plum-
ages. Not until the third year or later does the
bird seem to assume its full nuptial and adult
coloration.

When I first open my eyes on a bright midsummer morning, the first sound that becomes
part of my waking consciousness is the recurrent

rush and spill of the summer sea; then do I hear
a patter of tiny feet on the roof over my head
and the cheerful notes of a song sparrow's home-
spun tune. These sparrows are the songbirds of
the dunes. I hear them all day long, for I have a
pair nesting on the seaward slope of this dune in
a clump of dusty miller. My building of the
Fo'castle has given them something to sit on,
something they can see the world from, and on
its ridgepole they perch, singing at life in general
with a praiseworthy persistence. The bird really
has two songs, one the nuptial aria, the other
the domestic tune; it sings the first in the nest-
building, egg-laying season, and the second from
the close of the honeymoon to the silence in the
fall. I was amazed this year at the suddenness of
the change. On the afternoon of July 1st I heard
the birds on my roof singing aria number one;
on the morning of July 2d they had turned the
page to aria number two. The songs are alike;
they resemble each other in musical "shape,"
but the first is much more of a warble than the
second.

On throwing open my door on the dunes, the
morning sea, and the vast empty beach with its
coast guard paths, I find the house being stormed

by swallows—they are picking up the half-torpid flies that have spent the night on the shingles and just buzzed off—and on looking north and south along the dunes I see swallows everywhere. The grass glistens in the early morning light, the slant of the sun picks out the ripening spears, the graceful birds swim close above the green. Most of these birds are bank swallows, *Riparia riparia*, but I often see barn swallows, *Hirundo erythrogastra*, and tree swallows, *Iridoprocne bicolor*, scattered in among them. A little after seven o'clock they melt away. Through the day stray birds come foraging, but the swarm is a morning affair. The bank swallows (the bird with whitish underparts and a dark band across the breast) have nests north of Nauset Station in a clay stratum of the great bank; the tree swallows and the barn swallows live farther inland near the farms. Some say that the bank swallows nest in these dunes. I have never found their nests in this living sand, but the swallows may manage it, after all. Time and again have I been astounded at the manner in which animals use this sand as if it were ordinary earth. Not long ago, on the top of big dune, I found that moles had tunnelled a surface of live sand for six or seven feet.

The common tern, *Sterna hirundo*, here called the mackerel gull, dominates both the beach and the summer day. Three or four thousand of these birds are nesting in the region; there are nests on the dunes, and whole colonies on certain gravelly areas in the marsh islands near Orleans. All day long I watch them flying to and fro past my windows, now sailing with a favouring wind, now battling into an opposing breeze; I see them going along the breakers long before sunrise, white birds flying past a rosiness of eastern sky and an ocean still blue and dark with night; I see them pass like spiritual creatures in the dusk. There are crowded days when I live in a cloud of their wings and the clamour of their cries.

Sterna hirundo, the common tern—Wilson's tern, some call him—is indeed a lovely bird. His dominant colours are pearl-grey and white, his wings are bent, he is from thirteen to sixteen inches long, and he is marked by a black hood, an orange-coral bill tipped with black, and bright vermilion-orange legs and feet. To my ear, the bird's call has a cawing quality; it is, indeed, a cawing screech with an "e" sound and a high pitch. Harsh though it is, it is not disagreeable; moreover, it is capable of wide emotional variations. Going south on a recent day along the dunes, I arrived at the place where the parent terns, homing from the sea, were crossing the sand bar on their way to their nests, and as the birds came in sight of their mates and their fledglings, their cry changed its quality, and took on a kind of wild, harsh tenderness that was touching to hear.

On Monday morning last, as I sat writing at my west windows, I heard a tern give a strange cry, and on looking out and up I saw a bird harrying the female marsh hawk, of whose visits to the dunes I have already told. The sea bird's battle cry was entirely new to my ear. "*Ke'ke'ke'-aow!*" he cried; there was warning in the harsh, horny cry, danger and anger. The greater bird, flapping her wings as if they were spreads of paper—the winging of this hawk, near earth, is sometimes curiously like the winging of a butter-fly—made no answer, but sank to earth slowly, wings outspread, and rested for a long half minute on the shell-strewn floor of the sand pit forty feet back from my house. Thus perched motionless, she might have been a willing mark. Scolding without pause, the tern, who had followed the enemy down into the pit, then rose and dived on her as he might have dived on a fish. The hawk continued to sit motionless. It was an extraordinary scene. Regaining level wing just above the hawk's head, the tern instantly climbed and dived again. At his third dive, the hawk took off, flying ahead and low across the sand pit. The battle then moved into the dunes, and the last I saw of the affair was the hawk abandoning the hills and flying south unpursued far out over the marsh.

Watching the hawk thus a-squat on the sand in a summer intensity of light, with the grey sea bird angrily assailing her, there came into my mind a thought of the ancient Egyptian representations of animals and birds. For this hawk in the pit was the Horus Hawk of the Egyptians, the same poise, the same dark blood-fierceness, the same authority. The longer I live here and the more I see of birds and animals, the greater my admiration becomes for those artists who worked in Egypt so many long thousand years ago, drawing, painting, carving in the stifling quiet of the royal tombs, putting here ducks frightened out of the Nile marshes, here cattle being herded down a village street, here the great sun vulture, the jackal, and the snake. To my mind, no representations of animals equal these Egyptian renderings. I do not write in praise of faithful delineation or pictorial usage—though the Egyptian drew from his model with care—but of the unique power to reach, understand, and portray the very psyche of animals. The power is particularly notable in Egyptian representations of birds. A hawk of stone carved in hardest granite on a temple wall will have the soul of all hawks in his eyes. Moreover, there is nothing human about these Egyptian creatures. They are self-contained and aloof as becomes folk of a first and intenser world.

So completely do the thronging terns dominate the beach that they will often gather to chivvy off a human intruder. I am often chased all the way to Nauset. Three made for me yesterday afternoon as I was going north at two o'clock, trudging the hot and heavy sand.

It is an odd, a rather amusing experience to be thus barked at and chivvied along by birds. Down the beach they followed me, keeping pace with me and stopping when I stopped, their swallow-like tail feathers fish-tailing out as they manœuvred close above my head. About once every half minute one of the three would climb twenty or thirty feet above me and behind, tread air for a second or two, and then swoop directly down at me with a scolding cry, the rush ending in an up-lane scarce a foot above my head. So soundly was I scolded, and so constant was the sharp clamour, that one might have thought that the birds had found me pirating eggs and nestlings. As a matter of fact, I was miles away from any nest or nesting place. Those who disturb terns actually on their nests are chivvied by dozens in just such a manner, and are even struck, and struck vigorously, by the birds.

I suspect the marsh hawk of being on her way to raid these nests. Madam Hawk has probably been sitting on eggs of her own, for I have seen little of her since she gave up her daily forays sometime in the spring.

From mid-June to mid-July, the terns are at their best. Their eggs are hatching, the fish are running, and all day long the parent birds are going back and forth between their nests and the sea. When I open my door at sunrise, the terns

are already passing my house, flying twenty
or thirty feet above the curling, oncoming seas.
Hour by hour they pass in two endless streams,
one going fishing, the other bringing home the
catch; hour after hour they pass—thousands of
birds an hour when the fishing is good and near at
hand. Returning birds, almost without excep-
tion, hold silvery fish crosswise in their bills, and,
unlike the crow in the fable, a tern can cry out
without dropping his prize.

The great majority of these birds are males
bringing food to their mates and the new-born
young. The catch usually consists of three- and
four-inch sand eels, but I occasionally see birds
flying bow-down with tinker mackerel. Sometimes a bird passes carrying two "eels," holding
the pair as best he can.

A week ago, just after two o'clock on a bright
afternoon, the birds suddenly came streaming
from everywhere to the surf along the dunes.
Skates had again driven in a people of "eels."
It was high tide; the seas gathered and broke,
the heaviest shaking the beach. Into the curling
baroque crests of the waves, into the advancing
slopes of the gathering green swells, into the race
and flow of white seethe and yellow sand, the

bright air rained down birds on the now doubly imperilled and darting prey. The air was cut with wings and pierced with eager, hungry, and continuous cries. The birds make plummet dives and strike up jets of water from the surf. The harassed fish moving south, the terns followed after them; an hour later, through field glasses, I could see the thing still going on just north and seaward of the shoals.

Piratic jaegers, *Stercorarius pomarinus, Stercorarius parasiticus,* apparently never trouble these Eastham birds. I have seen but one jaeger on this beach, and that a solitary bird who chanced to pass the house one morning last September. Cape Cod neighbours, however, tell me that jaegers are numerous in the bay, and that they harry the terns who fish the shoals off Billingsgate.

Almost every day, in the full heat of noontide, I go down to the lower beach and lie down for a while on the hot sand, an arm over my eyes. The other day, in a spirit of fun, I raised my arm toward a passing tern—the returning birds fly scarce thirty feet above the beach—and to my amusement the creature paused, sank, and hovered above me for a few seconds scarce ten feet from my hand. I saw then that its under plumage, instead of being white, was a lovely faint rose; I had halted a roseate tern, *Sterna dougalli*. I wriggled my fingers; the bird responded with a cry in which I read bewildered indignation; then on it flew, and the incident ended.

This year a number of laughing gulls, *Larus atricilla*, accompany the terns fishing, the dozen or so gulls keeping to themselves while flying with their neighbours.

The most interesting adventure with birds I have had this summer I had with a flock of least terns, *Sterna antillarum*. It came to pass that early one morning in June, as I happened to be passing big dune, a covey of small terns unexpectedly sailed out at me and hovered about me, scolding and complaining. To my great delight, I saw that they were least terns or "tit gulls," rare creatures on our coast, and perhaps the prettiest and most graceful of summer's ocean birds. A miniature tern, the "leastie," scarce larger than a swallow, and you may know him by the lighter grey of his plumage, his bright lemon-yellow bill, and his delicate orange-yellow feet.

The birds were nesting at the foot of big dune,

and I had disturbed their peace. In the splendour of morning they hung above me, now uttering a single alarmed cheep, now a series of staccato cries.

I walked over to the nests.

The nest of such a beach bird is a singular affair. It is but a depression, and sometimes scarcely that, in the open, shelterless beach. "Nest building on the open sand," says Mr. Forbush, "is but the work of a moment. The bird alights, crouches slightly, and works its little feet so rapidly that the motion seems a mere blur, while the sand flies out in every direction as the creature pivots about. The tern then settles lower and smooths the cavity by turning and working and moving its body from side to side."

I have mislaid the scrap of paper on which I jotted down the number of nests I found that morning, but I think I counted twenty to twenty-five. There were eggs in every nest, in some two, in others three, in one case and one only, four. To describe the coloration of the shells is difficult, for there was a deal of variation, but perhaps I can give some idea of their appearance by saying that they were beach-coloured with overtones of bluish green, and speckled with browns and violet-browns and lavenders. What interested me most, however, was not the eggs, but the manner in which the birds had decorated their nests with pebbles and bits of shell. Here and there along the beach, the "leasties" had picked up flat bits of sea shell about the size of a finger nail, and with these bits they had lined the bowl of their nests, setting the flat pieces in flat, like parts of a mosaic.

For two weeks I watched these "leasties" and their nests, taking every precaution not to disturb or alarm the setting birds. Yet I had but to pass anywhere between them and the tide to put them up, and when I walked south with coast guardsmen, I heard single cries of alarm in the starry and enormous night. Toward the end of June, a sudden northeaster came.

It was a night storm. I built a little fire, wrote a letter or two, and listened to the howling wind and the bursts of rain. All night long, and it was a wakeful, noisy night, I had the "leasties" on my mind. I felt them out there on the wild shelterless beach, with the black gale screaming over them and the rain pouring down. Opening my door, I looked for a moment into the drenching blackness and heard a great roaring of the sea.

The tide and the gale had ebbed together when I rose at five the next morning, but there was still wind and a grey drizzle. At the foot of big dune I found desolation. The tide had swept the beach. Not a nest remained or a sign of a nest, and the birds had gone. Later that day, just south of big dune, I saw bits of bluish-green egg-shell in a lump of fresh weed. Where the birds went to, I never knew. Probably to a better place to try again.

Bless me! I thought, returning; what of the song sparrows?

Through the drenching grass, bare-legged, I hurried to the dusty-miller bush. The sand had been moving during the night; it had crept along the dunes, it had rained down with the drops of rain, and the bush was now well embedded. Indeed, it was a bush no more, but a thicket of separate stalks growing out of a deep, rain-soaked mound of sand. As I drew close to it, I saw through the rain the prudent eye of Madam Sparrow aglint in the leaves. The sand had risen to within an inch of her nest, the leaves which concealed it were awry with wind and choked with sand, but there sat the little bird, resolved and dutiful. She raised her brood—how well she deserved to—and some time in July the whole family moved out into the dunes.

I must now add a paragraph from my autumnal notes and tell of my last sight of the great summer throng of terns. It was an unforgettable experience. During August the birds thinned out, and as the month drew to a close, whole days passed without a sight or sign of their presence. By September 1st, I imagined that most of them had gone. Then came the unexpected. On Saturday, September 3d, friends came down the beach to see me, and at the close of their visit, as I opened the Fo'castle door, I found that the air above the dunes was snowy with young terns. The day had been mild, and the late afternoon light was mild and rosy golden—the sun was an hour from his setting—and high in space and golden light the myriads of birds drifted and whirled like leaves. North and south we saw them for miles along the dunes. For twenty minutes, perhaps, or half an hour, the swarming filled my sky, and during all that time I did not hear a single bird utter a single sound.

At the end of that period, withdrawing south and inland, the gathering melted away.

It was really a very curious thing. Apparently

some impulse from heaven had suddenly seized upon the birds, entered into their feathered breasts, and led them into the air above the dunes. Whence came that spirit, whence its will, and how had it breathed its purpose into those thousand hearts? The whole performance reminded me very much of a swarming of bees. A migrational impulse, yes, and something more. The birds were flying high, higher than I had ever seen terns go, and as far as I could judge—or guess—the great majority of the fliers were young birds of the year. It was a rapture, a glory of the young. And this was the last of the terns.

Late August, and day by day, I see more shore birds and see them oftener. All summer long there have been sandpipers and ringnecks on the beach, but earlier in the season the birds are elusive and may disappear for days. The first great flocks to return from the Northern breeding grounds arrived here about the middle of July. I remember their coming. For four interminable days a strong and tireless southwest wind had billowed across the lagoon and off to a smoky sea; on the morning of the fifth day, just before sunrise, this wind had died; then had come dullness and quiet, and, between nine and ten o'clock, a breath of easterly air. All that fifth afternoon the beach had been black with birds, most of them ringnecks or semipalmated plovers. The long southwester had apparently dammed up a great migrational stream. These first flocks were vagrant mobs. Walking to Nauset between two and three o'clock, I must have put up between two and three thousand birds. As I drew near, mob after mob after mob crowded the air and sought feeding grounds ahead. The smaller autumnal flocks had flown in psychic unity, rising and falling, wheeling and alighting together; these mobs scattered and divided into wandering companies.

Late August, and my wild ducks, having raised their families, are returning by hundreds to the marsh. During May and June and early July, when I wandered about this region in the night, I heard no sound from the flats. Now, when I get out to signal to the first coast guardsman coming south at half-past nine, I heard from the dark levels a sentinel quack, a call. The marsh fills with life again; the great sun goes south along green treetops and moorlands fruiting and burned brown.

The quality of life, which in the ardour of

spring was personal and sexual, becomes social in midsummer. Stirred by the vernal fire, a group psychically dissolves, for every creature in a flock is intent upon the use and the offering of his own awakened flesh. Even creatures who are of the flocking or herding habit emerge as individuals. With the rearing of the young, and their integration into the reëstablished group, life becomes again a social rhythm. The body has been given and sacrificially broken, its own gods and all gods obeyed.

IV

The other day I saw a young swimmer in the surf. He was, I judged, about twenty-two years old and a little less than six feet tall, splendidly built, and as he stripped I saw that he must have been swimming since the season began, for he was sunburned and brown. Standing naked on the steep beach, his feet in the climbing seethe, he gathered himself for a swimmer's crouching spring, watched his opportunity, and suddenly leaped headfirst through a long arc of air into the wall of a towering and enormous wave. Again and again he repeated his jest, emerging each time beyond the breaker with a stare of salty eyes, a shake of the head, and a smile. It was all a beautiful thing to see: the surf thundering across the great natural world, the beautiful and compact body in its naked strength and symmetry, the astounding plunge across the air, arms extended ahead, legs and feet together, the emerging stroke of the flat hands, and the alternate rhythms of the sunburned and powerful shoulders.

Watching this picture of a fine human being free for the moment of everything save his own humanity and framed in a scene of nature, I could not help musing on the mystery of the human body and of how nothing can equal its rich and rhythmic beauty when it is beautiful or approach its forlorn and pathetic ugliness when beauty has not been mingled in or has withdrawn. Poor body, time and the long years were the first tailors to teach you the merciful use of clothes! Though some scold to-day because you are too much seen, to my mind, you are not seen fully enough or often enough when you are beautiful. All my life it has given me pleasure to see beautiful human beings. To see beautiful young men and women gives one a kind of reverence for humanity (alas, of how few experiences may this

be said), and surely there are few moods of the
spirit more worthy of our care than those in
which we reverence, even for a moment, our
tragic and bewildered kind.

My swimmer having gone his way, out of a
chance curiosity I picked the top of a dune
goldenrod, and found at the very bottom of a
cocoon of twisted leaves the embryo head of the
late autumnal flower.

Chapter X

ORION RISES ON THE DUNES

So came August to its close, ending its last day with a night so luminous and still that a mood came over me to sleep out on the open beach under the stars. There are nights in summer when darkness and ebbing tide quiet the universal wind, and this August night was full of that quiet of absence, and the sky was clear. South of my house, between the bold fan of a dune and the wall of a plateau, a sheltered hollow opens seaward, and to this nook I went, shouldering my blankets sailorwise. In the star-shine the hollow was darker than the immense and solitary beach, and its floor was still pleasantly warm with the overflow of day.

I fell asleep uneasily, and woke again as one wakes out-of-doors. The vague walls about me breathed a pleasant smell of sand, there was no sound, and the broken circle of grass above was as motionless as something in a house. Waking

218

again, hours afterward, I felt the air grown colder and heard a little advancing noise of waves. It was still night. Sleep gone and past recapture, I drew on my clothes and went to the beach. In the luminous east, two great stars aslant were rising clear of the exhalations of darkness gathered at the rim of night and ocean—Betelgeuse and Bellatrix, the shoulders of Orion. Autumn had come, and the Giant stood again at the horizon of day and the ebbing year, his belt still hidden in the bank of cloud, his feet in the deeps of space and the far surges of the sea.

My year upon the beach had come full circle; it was time to close my door. Seeing the great suns, I thought of the last time I marked them in the spring, in the April west above the moors, dying into the light and sinking. I saw them of old above the iron waves of black December, sparkling afar. Now, once again, the Hunter rose to drive summer south before him, once again autumn followed on his steps. I had seen the ritual of the sun; I had shared the elemental world. Wraiths of memories began to take shape. I saw the sleet of the great storm slanting down again into the grass under the thin seepage of moon, the blue-white spill of an immense billow on the outer bar, the swans in the high October sky, the sunset madness and splendour of the year's terns over the dunes, the clouds of beach birds arriving, the eagle solitary in the blue. And because I had known this outer and secret world, and been able to live as I had lived, reverence and gratitude greater and deeper than ever possessed me, sweeping every emotion else aside, and space and silence an instant closed together over life. Then time gathered again like a cloud, and presently the stars began to pale over an ocean still dark with remembered night.

During the months that have passed since that September morning some have asked me what understanding of Nature one shapes from so strange a year? I would answer that one's first appreciation is a sense that the creation is still going on, that the creative forces are as great and as active to-day as they have ever been, and that to-morrow's morning will be as heroic as any of the world. *Creation is here and now.* So near is man to the creative pageant, so much a part is he of the endless and incredible experiment, that any glimpse he may have will be but the revelation of a moment, a solitary note heard in a symphony thundering through debatable exist-

ences of time. Poetry is as necessary to comprehension as science. It is as impossible to live
without reverence as it is without joy.

And what of Nature itself, you say—that cal-
lous and cruel engine, red in tooth and fang?
Well, it is not so much of an engine as you think.
As for "red in tooth and fang," whenever I hear
the phrase or its intellectual echoes I know that
some passer-by has been getting life from books. It
is true that there are grim arrangements. Beware
of judging them by whatever human values are
in style. As well expect Nature to answer to your
human values as to come into your house and
sit in a chair. The economy of nature, its checks
and balances, its measurements of competing
life—all this is its great marvel and has an ethic
of its own. Live in Nature, and you will soon see
that for all its non-human rhythm, it is no cave
of pain. As I write I think of my beloved birds
of the great beach, and of their beauty and their
zest of living. And if there are fears, know also
that Nature has its unexpected and unappreci-
ated mercies.

Whatever attitude to human existence you
fashion for yourself, know that it is valid only
if it be the shadow of an attitude to Nature. A

human life, so often likened to a spectacle upon a stage, is more justly a ritual. The ancient values of dignity, beauty, and poetry which sustain it are of Nature's inspiration; they are born of the mystery and beauty of the world. Do no dishonour to the earth lest you dishonour the spirit of man. Hold your hands out over the earth as over a flame. To all who love her, who open to her the doors of their veins, she gives of her strength, sustaining them with her own measureless tremor of dark life. Touch the earth, love the earth, honour the earth, her plains, her valleys, her hills, and her seas; rest your spirit in her solitary places. For the gifts of life are the earth's and they are given to all, and they are the songs of birds at daybreak, Orion and the Bear, and dawn seen over ocean from the beach.

THE END